THE MARSHALL CAVENDISH
☆ ☆ ☆ ILLUSTRATED ☆ ☆ ☆
ENCYCLOPEDIA OF
WORLD WAR II

VOLUME 18

THE MARSHALL CAVENDISH
☆ ☆ ☆ ILLUSTRATED ☆ ☆ ☆
ENCYCLOPEDIA OF
WORLD WAR II

Based on the original text by
Lieutenant Colonel Eddy Bauer

CONSULTANT EDITOR

Brigadier General James L. Collins, Jr., U.S.A.
CHIEF OF MILITARY HISTORY, DEPARTMENT OF THE ARMY

MARSHALL CAVENDISH CORPORATION/NEW YORK

CONTENTS

Editorial Director: Brian Innes
Editor-in-chief; Brigadier Peter Young, D.S.O., M.C., M.A.
Managing Editor: Richard Humble
Editor: Christopher Chant
Art Editor: Jim Bridge

CHAPTER 151
Victory in Europe

Over the 30 miles of the Küstrin bridge-head, the attack started at 0400 hours, lit up by 143 searchlights. Five armies, including the 1st Guards Tank Army, took part in it, but this concentration did not favour the attack, which had only advanced between two and five miles by the end of the day. In the Frankfurt sector, Zhukov's successes were even more modest. Nevertheless, on the first day, O.K.W. had to hand over LVI Panzer Corps (General Weidling) to Busse, who put it between XI S.S. and LI Corps.

On the Neisse, between Forst and Muskau, the troops of the 1st Ukrainian Front had had a better day. At 0655 hours the engineers had already thrown a bridge across this 130-foot wide obstacle so that at nightfall Konev had a bridgehead which was eight miles deep in places on a 16-mile front. The 4th *Panzerarmee* (General F.-H. Gräser) was more than half shattered, which appeared to con-firm the soundness of Hitler's instinct in

showing him that the enemy's main effort would bear on Dresden rather than Ber-lin; this was his last victory over his Intelligence service.

For three whole days attacks and coun-ter-attacks followed each other on the Oder's left bank to a depth of nine miles. German supplies brought up towards the line were stopped by the ceaseless attacks of countless Soviet fighter-bombers. But Zhukov had suffered heavy losses and Hitler was confident that at a daily rate of loss of 250 T-34's and JS-3's, the enemy offensive would finally become exhausted. But again Busse, to stop the gaps which were opening every day along his front, was in the position of a player forced to throw down his last chips onto the table: LVI Panzer Corps, 25th and 18th *Panzer-grenadier*, "Nordland" and "Nederland" Panzer Divisions; and the defeat of the 4th *Panzerarmee*, which became more and more complete, threatened his communications.

△ *The culmination of Russia's enormous war effort: the Red flag flies over the ruins of Berlin. The Red Army's last offensive had been crowned by success – but only at a terrible cost.*

△ *The general staff of the 1st Belorussian Front in session during the preparatory stages of the planning for the Berlin operation. The 1st Belorussian Front had the major task in this last offensive, that of sweeping down from the north and crushing the German capital's defences, but in the event Zhukov had to summon Konev's 1st Ukrainian Front to his aid from the south.*

April 19: day of decision

April 19 was the decisive day on the Oder front: on that day the German 9th Army disintegrated. LI Corps, which was thrown back against Eberswalde, lost all contact with LVI Panzer Corps, which was itself cut off from XI S.S. Corps; through this last breach Zhukov managed to reach Strausberg, which was about 22 miles from the New Chancellery bunker.

On the same day Konev, on the 1st Ukrainian Front, was already exploiting the situation; he crossed the Spree at Spremberg and penetrated Saxon territory at Bautzen and Hoyerswerda. The *Stavka*, which was not satisfied with Zhukov's manner of conducting his battle, urged Konev to carry out the alternative plan previously discussed.

For the last time, Hitler's dispositions favoured the enemy. Certainly neither Heinrici nor Busse opposed LI Corps' attachment to the 3rd *Panzerarmee,* but the order given to LVI Panzer Corps to reinforce the Berlin garrison without allowing the 9th Army to pull back from the Oder appeared madness to them: outflanked on its right by Konev's impetuous thrust, it was also exposed on its left. But, as always, the Führer remained deaf to these sensible objections, and Busse received the imperious order to counter-attack the 1st Ukrainian Front's columns from the north whilst Gräser

attacked them from the south.

The result was that on April 22, the 1st Guards Tank Army (1st Belorussian Front), leaving the Berlin region to its north-west, identified at Königs Wusterhausen the advance guard of the 3rd Guards Tank Army (1st Ukrainian Front) which, executing Stalin's latest instruction, had veered from the west to the north from Finsterwalde. The circle had therefore closed around the German 9th Army. That evening, Lelyushenko's armoured forces pushed forward to Jüterborg, cutting the Berlin–Dresden road, whilst Zhukov, advancing through Bernau, Wandlitz, Oranienburg, and Birkenwerder (which had fallen to Lieutenant-General F. I. Perkhorovich's 47th Army and Colonel-General N. E. Berzarin's 5th Shock Army) cut the Berlin–Stettin and Berlin–Stralsund roads. The encirclement of the capital, therefore, was completed two days later when the 8th Guards and 4th Guards Tank Armies linked up in Ketzin.

Hitler's last throw

Hitler refused to abandon the city and insisted on taking personal charge of its defence. He had a little more than 90,000 men at his disposal, including the youths and 50-year-old men of the *Volkssturm,* as well as the remainder of LVI Panzer Corps. But in spite of this he did not regard

sive launched on April 20 against the 3rd *Panzerarmee* by Rokossovsky across the lower Oder. Elsewhere, as Zhukov spread out towards the west, Steiner was compelled to thin out his forces even more, some of which were entirely worn out and the rest badly undertrained. Finally on April 26, the troops of the 2nd Belorussian Front, after making a breach below Schwedt, moved towards Prenzlau. Heinrici withdrew two or three divisions from the 11th Army to stop them. As he was unable to have him shot for insubordination, Keitel could only relieve him of his command. In the present position, he would have found no one to pronounce a death sentence and have it carried out.

Meanwhile, Hitler had addressed the following order of the day to the 12th Army on April 23: "Soldiers of the Wenck Army! An immensely important order requires you to withdraw from the combat zone against our enemies in the

the battle as lost. Whilst he galvanised the resistance, Field-Marshal Keitel and Colonel-General Jodl, who had both left Berlin on his instructions, would mount the counter-attacks which would complete the enemy's defeat. The 11th Army (General F. Steiner) would emerge from the Oranienburg–Eberswalde front and crush Zhukov against the north front of the capital whilst Konev, on the south front, would meet the same fate from General W. Wenck and his 12th Army. Meanwhile, the Brandenburg *Gauleiter,* Joseph Goebbels, launched into inflammatory speeches and bloodthirsty orders:

"Your Gauleiter is with you," he shouted through the microphone, "he swears that he will of course remain in your midst with his colleagues. His wife and children are also here. He who once conquered this city with 200 men will henceforth organise the defence of the capital by all possible means." And these were the means: "Any man found not doing his duty," he decreed, "will be hanged on a lamp post after a summary judgement. Moreover, placards will be attached to the corpses stating: 'I have been hanged here because I am too cowardly to defend the capital of the Reich'–'I have been hanged because I did not believe in the Führer'–'I am a deserter and for this reason I shall not see this turning-point of destiny'." etc.

The 11th Army's counter-attack never materialised, mainly because of the offen-

guns roaring. The Führer calls you! You are getting ready for the attack as before in the time of your victories. Berlin is waiting for you!"

The German 12th Army gave way to the Western Allies on the Elbe between Wittenberge and Wittenberg and carried out the regrouping and change of front prescribed. With a strength of two Panzer corps and a handful of incomplete and hastily trained divisions it moved on Berlin. During this forward movement, which brought it to Belzig, 30 miles from the bunker where Hitler was raging and fuming, it picked up the Potsdam garrison and the remnants of the 9th Army (estimated at 40,000 men), who had with great difficulty made their way from Lübben to Zossen, leaving more than 200,000 dead, wounded, and prisoners and almost all its *matériel* behind it. On April 29, however, Wenck was compelled to note that this last sudden effort had finished the 12th Army, and that it could no longer hold its positions.

In Berlin, the armies of the 1st Belorussian Front started to round on the last centres of resistance on the same day. A tremendous artillery force, under Marshal Voronov, supported the infantry's attacks. It had 25,000 guns and delivered, according to some reports, 25,600 tons of shells against the besieged city, that is, in less than a week, more than half the 45,517 tons of bombs which British and American planes had dropped on the German capital since August 25, 1940.

April 30: Hitler commits suicide

When he heard of Steiner's inability to counter-attack, Hitler flew into an uncontrollable fury; and Wenck's defeat left him with no alternative but captivity or death. In the meantime he had dismissed Hermann Göring and Heinrich Himmler from the Party, depriving them of all their offices, the former for attempting to assume power after the blockade of Berlin, the latter for trying to negotiate a cease-fire with the Western powers through Count Folke Bernadotte. On the evening of April 28, he married Eva Braun, whose brother-in-law he had just had shot for abandoning his post, made his will on the next day with Joseph Goebbels, Martin Bormann, and Generals Burgdorf

△ *Marshal of the Soviet Union I.S. Konev, commander of the 1st Ukrainian front fighting its way westwards south of Berlin.*
△▷▷ *German troops try to rescue as much as they can from a burning S.S. vehicle outside the Anhalter Station in Berlin.*
△▷ *Part of the final exodus from the doomed capital.*
▷ *Berliners flee their homes muffled and goggled against the dust and smoke of the last battle. Overleaf: Soviet troops wild with delight after the fall of the Reichstag.*

West and march East. Your mission is simple. Berlin must remain German. You must at all costs reach your planned objectives, for other operations are also in hand, designed to deal a decisive blow against the Bolsheviks in the struggle for the capital of the Reich and so to reverse the position in Germany. Berlin will never capitulate to Bolshevism. The defenders of the Reich's capital have regained their courage on hearing of your rapid approach; they are fighting bravely and stubbornly, and are firmly convinced that they will soon hear your and Krebs as witnesses, and committed suicide a little before 1600 hours on April 30, probably by firing his revolver at his right temple.

Much has been written about Hitler's disappearance and the various places of refuge that he reached outside Germany. But in fact Marshal Sokolovsky, the former chief-of-staff of the 1st Belorussian Front who was interviewed by Cornelius Ryan in Moscow on April 17, 1963, admitted to him that the Führer's body had been unmistakably identified by his dentist's assistants early in May 1945. Nevertheless on May 26 Stalin, who must have known this fact, assured Harry Hopkins that in his opinion Hitler was not dead and that he was hiding somewhere. When Hopkins put forward the suggestion that Hitler had escaped to a U-Boat Stalin added, according to the account of this meeting, that "this was done with the connivance of Switzerland."

May 2: Berlin falls

On May 2, 1945, after Generals Krebs and Burgdorf had also committed suicide, General H. Weidling surrendered to Chuikov, the heroic defender of Stalingrad, all that remained of the Berlin garrison, about 70,000 totally exhausted men.

▷ *Tank-eye view of the approach to the* Reichstag.

▽ *A Russian Stalin 3 heavy tank co-operates with infantry during the savage and costly house-to-house fighting for Berlin.*

Zhukov's crushing victory should not, however, appear to overshadow the equally significant successes obtained by Konev over Schörner, whom Hitler had at the eleventh hour promoted to Field-Marshal. Having routed the 4th *Panzer-armee,* Konev went on to occupy the ruins of Dresden after a last engagement at Kamenz. Two days later, his 5th Guards Army (General Zhadov) established its first contact with the American 1st Army, whilst Marshal Rybalko and General Lelyushenko's forces made off towards Prague, whose population rose up against their German "protectors" on May 4. Army Group "Centre", which had about 50 divisions, was now cut off from its communications.

Germany surrenders . . .

Grand-Admiral Dönitz, who had been invested by Hitler's last will with supreme power over what remained of Germany, now had to put an end to this war in conditions which Kaiser Wilhelm II, unbalanced as he was and a mediocre politician and strategist, had managed to spare his empire and his subjects in November 1918. In his attempt to finish off the war, the new head of state tried to save the largest possible number of German troops from Soviet captivity, and was quite ready to let the British and Americans take them prisoner.

. . . on May 3 on Lüneburg Heath . . .

On May 3, General E. Kinzel, Field-Marshal Busch's chief-of-staff, and Admiral H.-G. von Friedeburg, new head of the Kriegsmarine, presented themselves on Lüneburg Heath to Field-Marshal Montgomery and offered him the surrender of the German forces in the north of Germany, including those retreating from Marshal Rokossovsky.

They were dismissed, and on May 4, at 1820 hours, they had to accede to the conditions stipulated in Eisenhower's name by Montgomery. The instrument they signed now only related to the land and sea forces opposed to the 21st Army Group in the Netherlands, in north-west Germany, in the Friesian Islands, in

The German *Sturmmörser* Tiger heavy assault vehicle

Weight: 70 tons.
Crew: 7.
Armament: one 38-cm *Raketenwerfer* 61 rocket projector with 12 projectiles and one 7.92-mm MG 34 machine gun.
Armour: hull nose and front plate 100-mm, rear 82-mm, upper sides 80-mm, lower sides 60-mm, and belly 26-mm; superstructure front 150-mm, sides and rear 84-mm, and roof 40-mm.
Engine: one Maybach HL 230 P45 inline, 700-hp.
Speed: 25 mph on roads and 15 mph cross-country.
Range: 87 miles on roads and 55 miles cross-country.
Length: 20 feet 8½ inches.
Width: 12 feet 3 inches.
Height: 11 feet 4 inches.

The German forces in the north surrender to Field-Marshal Montgomery at Lüneburg Heath.
▷ The German delegation arrives at Montgomery's headquarters. This party had been sent by Keitel with the permission of Dönitz, who had been appointed head of state by Hitler's will. The delegation's members were, from left to right, Admiral Friedeburg, C.-in-C. German Navy, General Kinzel, chief-of-staff to Field-Marshal Busch, Rear-Admiral Wagner, and Major Freidel. Montgomery sent them away with a demand for unconditional surrender.
▽ The surrender delegation arrives on May 4.
▽▷ General Kinzel puts his signature to the surrender document.
▷▷ The seal is put on Germany's defeat in the north: Montgomery signs the surrender at 1830 hours on May 4, 1945.

Heligoland, and in Schleswig-Holstein. In spite of this fair dealing, the Russians occupied the Danish island of Bornholm.

. . . on May 7 at Rheims . . .

General Eisenhower kept to the same principle in the surrender document which put an end to the European war at 0241 hours on May 7, 1941. This merciless war had lasted a little over 68 months.

When he received the German delegation in the Rheims school which housed S.H.A.E.F., Lieutenant-General Walter Bedell Smith, Eisenhower's chief-of-staff, read out the document decided by the Allies. It ordered the simultaneous cessation of hostilities on all fronts on May 8 at 2301 hours, confirmed the total defeat of the armed forces of the Third Reich, and settled the procedure for their surrender according to the principles governing the surrender on Lüneburg Heath. Colonel-General Jodl, General Admiral Friedeburg, and Major Oxenius of the Luftwaffe signed the surrender document in Germany's name. After Bedell Smith, Lieutenant-General Sir Frederick Morgan signed for Great Britain, General Sévez for France, and Major-General Susloparov for the U.S.S.R. Finally Lieutenant-General Carl A. Spaatz, Vice-Admiral Sir Harold M. Burrough, and Air-Marshal Sir J. M. Robb signed for the U.S. Air Force, the Royal Navy, and the R.A.F. respectively.

. . . and on May 8 in Berlin

The following day, Air Chief-Marshal Sir Arthur Tedder, as Eisenhower's deputy, flew to Berlin accompanied by General Spaatz for the final act of the Wehrmacht's and the Third Reich's unconditional surrender. The ceremony took place at the 1st Belorussian Front's H.Q. Field-Marshal Keitel, Admiral Friedeburg, and Colonel-General Stumpff, who signed for the Luftwaffe, appeared before Marshal Zhukov, General de Lattre de Tassigny, and the two previously mentioned officers at 0028 hours. On May 8 the European part of World War II ended.

The surrender of the German forces, with the exception of Army Group

The American Bell P-63A Kingcobra fighter and fighter-bomber

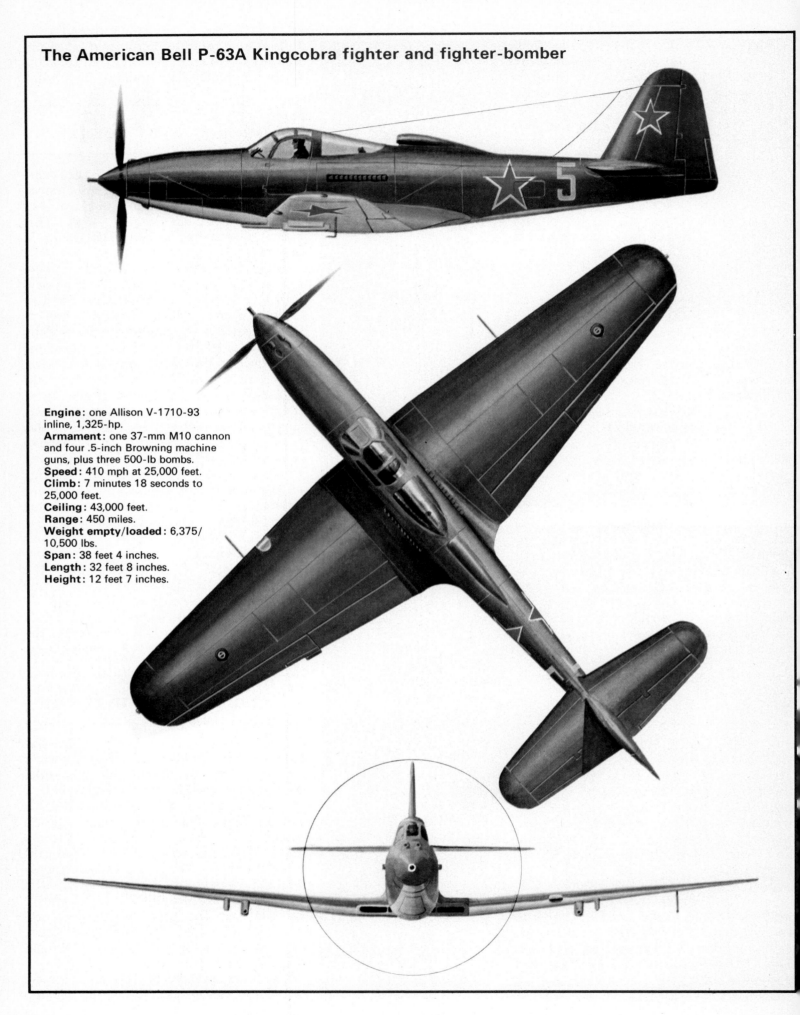

Engine: one Allison V-1710-93 inline, 1,325-hp.
Armament: one 37-mm M10 cannon and four .5-inch Browning machine guns, plus three 500-lb bombs.
Speed: 410 mph at 25,000 feet.
Climb: 7 minutes 18 seconds to 25,000 feet.
Ceiling: 43,000 feet.
Range: 450 miles.
Weight empty/loaded: 6,375/ 10,500 lbs.
Span: 38 feet 4 inches.
Length: 32 feet 8 inches.
Height: 12 feet 7 inches.

"Centre", took place at the time specified. Wireless communication was irregular between Flensburg, the seat of Dönitz's government, and Josefov in Bohemia, where Schörner had set up his last H.Q. In any event, this last corner of German resistance had given up the struggle by May 10.

In the period between the various stages of surrender, though it was brief, hundreds of thousands of Wehrmacht soldiers, even on the other side of the Elbe, managed to get past Montgomery's and Bradley's advance guards and surrender to the Western Allies. The Kriegsmarine also made full use of its last hours of freedom and as far as it could evacuated its Baltic positions.

Finally Colonel-General C. Hilpert, commander of Army Group "Kurland" since his colleague Rendulic's sudden transfer to Austria, handed over to the Russians a little less than 200,000 men, what was left of his two armies (five corps or 16 divisions). Similarly General Noak surrendered XX Corps (7th, 32nd, and 239th Divisions) which still held the Hela peninsula and the mouth of the Vistula. The German 20th Army, occupying Norway with five corps of 14 divisions (400,000 men and 100,000 Soviet prisoners) surrendered at Oslo to Lieutenant-General Sir Alfred Thorne. The 319th Division abandoned its pointless occupation in the Channel Islands, as did the garrisons at Dunkirk, Lorient, and Saint Nazaire; finally the surrender at Rheims saved la Rochelle from the tragic fate that had befallen Royan.

Allied Control Commission

On the following June 4, at Berlin, Marshal Zhukov, Field-Marshal Montgomery, and Generals Eisenhower and de Lattre de Tassigny approved four agreements governing Germany's disarmament, occupation, and administration, and decreeing that the principal Nazi war leaders should appear before an international court of military justice. It should be noted with reference to these agreements that as they were not in a position to prejudge the territorial decisions of the future peace conference, the four contracting parties defined Germany as the Reich within its frontiers of December 1937.

During the last weeks of their furious

pursuit, Montgomery had advanced from Wismar on the Baltic to the Elbe just below Wittenberge, and General Bradley had reached the right bank of the Elbe as far as Torgau and to the south beyond Chemnitz (now Karl Marx Stadt). Both had gone beyond the limits set out in the Yalta agreements about the British, American, and Soviet occupation zones. Montgomery had gone about 45 miles ahead, Bradley about 125 miles. In fact, in the interests of their common victory, and without arousing the Kremlin's protests, the British and the Americans had exercised their "right of pursuit" beyond the demarcation line. Nevertheless on the day after the Rheims and Berlin surrenders, Stalin insisted on the precise implementation of all the promises given.

△ *A Russian points out to a party of British troops the spot where the bodies of Adolf Hitler and his last-minute wife, Eva Braun, were burned after their suicide on April 30.*

▽ *The victors: British and Russian officers inspect tanks of the 8th Hussars in Berlin. At the front, with Montgomery, are Marshals Zhukov and Rokossovsky, whom the British field-marshal had just invested with the Grand Cross of the Order of the Bath and Knight Commander of the Order of the Bath respectively.*

The end of the road for Nazi Germany.

△ *The Allied delegation at the surrender ceremony at Rheims. Lieutenant-General Walter Bedell Smith signs for Eisenhower, who refused to be present.*

△▷ *Colonel-General Jodl signs for the German high command.*

▷ △ *Nazi Germany's last Führer, Grand-Admiral Karl Dönitz (centre) with Dr. Albert Speer and Colonel General Alfred Jodl at the time of their arrest in May 1945.*

▷ ▽ *Field-Marshal Wilhelm Keitel ratifies the surrender document of May 8 early in the morning of May 9.*

But had he kept his own promises about the constitution of a Polish government in which the various democratic factions of the nation would be represented? In London it was well known that the Soviet secret services were systematically destroying all elements opposed to the setting up of a communist régime in Poland loyal to Moscow, and that in the Kremlin the commission established by the Yalta agreements to carry out the reorganisation of the government was paralysed by Molotov's obstruction.

In these circumstances, Churchill offered the opinion that the British and American armies should continue to occupy the positions they had reached in Germany up to the time when the coming conference of the Big Three in Berlin had clarified the situation. He also thought that this conference, which was first arranged for July 15, should be held earlier. For this reason he wrote to President Truman on June 4:

"I am sure you understand the reason why I am anxious for an earlier date, say 3rd or 4th (of July). I view with profound misgivings the retreat of the American Army to our line of occupation in the central sector, thus bringing Soviet power into the heart of Western Europe and the descent of the iron curtain between us and everything to the eastward. I hoped that this retreat, if it has to be made, would be accompanied by the settlement of many great things which would be the true foundation of world peace. Nothing really important has been settled yet, and you and I will have to bear great responsibility for the future. I still hope therefore that the date will be advanced."

On June 9, arguing that the Soviet occupation authorities' behaviour in Austria and the increasing number of irregularities against the missions of the Western powers justified his position, he returned to the charge:

"Would it not be better to refuse to withdraw on the main European front until a settlement has been reached about

Austria? Surely at the very least the whole agreement about zones should be carried out at the same time?"

The Russians move in

Harry Truman turned a deaf ear to these arguments and Churchill was informed that the American troops' retreat to the demarcation line would begin on June 21 and that the military chiefs would settle questions about the quadripartite occupation of Berlin and free access to the capital by air, rail, and road between them. This was done and on July 15, when the Potsdam conference began, the Red Army had set up its advanced positions 30 miles from the centre of Hamburg, within artillery range of Kassel, and less than 80 miles from Mainz on the Rhine.

It was a "fateful decision", Churchill wrote.

Prisoners of war: the lost armies

The mobile type of warfare of World War II often made it impossible for outnumbered land forces to be extricated, and left them no alternative to destruction but surrender. It was thus that millions of able-bodied soldiers, in addition to seriously wounded, were taken prisoner between 1939 and 1945.

The rights of prisoners-of-war were fully safeguarded by the Geneva Convention of 1929, a copy of which was displayed in every P.O.W. camp, or should have been. The protecting power, a neutral government appointed by a belligerent to look after its interests in enemy territory until the restoration of normal diplomatic relations, was entrusted with control of P.O.W. camps, and authorised to send delegates to visit camps and investigate complaints. The International Committee of the Red Cross also had the right to visit camps, and these visits soon became established as regular practice. Article 79 of the Convention entitled the International Committee to propose to the belligerent powers the organisation of a Central Information Agency for the reception, recording, and forwarding of information and replies to enquiries about prisoners-of-war. The Agency was established in September 1939.

But not all nations were signatories to the Convention. Japan had signed but not ratified it and was not, therefore, bound by its terms. The Japanese Government declared, however, shortly before entering the war in December 1941, that it would apply the provision *mutatis mutandis* to all prisoners-of-war, and, subject to reciprocity, non-combatant internees of enemy countries. The Red Cross Societies of the Allies and the International Committee were thus led to expect that they would be granted the same facilities to carry out their work as in other countries. But they were mistaken. The Committee's office in Tokyo was regarded with suspicion by the Japanese, and the work of the delegates was tolerated rather then permitted. Their mail was censored, delayed, and withheld. They had to obtain permits to visit camps and reasons were often found to cancel or delay visits. They were not notified of the existence of a great many camps and never obtained a complete list of prisoners.

1

1. German prisoners-of-war in a British camp. Extensive use was made in Britain during both World Wars of large country houses as prisoner-of-war camps. Many such houses were situated in remote rural areas, from which it would be relatively difficult to escape.

2. An early prisoner: a German airman captured in August 1940 during the Battle of Britain enjoys a drink provided by his captors, a warden, a policeman, and men of the Royal Army Service Corps.

3. Survivors from a U-boat sunk by British naval units await transport to a camp on the quayside.

Russia applied the terms of The Hague Regulations of 1907 (which the Geneva Convention superseded), according to which each belligerent state set up an information bureau to answer enquiries. The transmission of a nominal roll was not stipulated nor any mention made of the Central Agency. The Soviet Union, in fact, shrouded its actions in mystery. Consequently, Germany received no information regarding troops captured by the Russians, and ceased to transmit lists of Russian prisoners, or to allow camp visits to them, although the state of Russian prisoners in Germany greatly concerned the International Committee. In Germany, the Committee's delegates visited camps for prisoners of all countries except Russia.

The enormous variety of camp conditions and of individual experiences makes difficult any wide generalisation regarding P.O.W.s. Conditions varied in different countries and, inside these countries, in different camps at different periods of the war, quite often according to the personality of the camp commandant. The local supplies of food, water, and medicine as well as local conditions of heat, cold, and dampness all had influence. In general it may be said that prisoner conditions in the Far East were more damaging to health than those in Europe.

Accommodation for P.O.W.s was limited and of varying quality. Allied troops captured in North Africa often waited months in transit camps, in very poor conditions, spending days in crowded trucks, and nights herded into wire pens. Many contracted dysentery, and were weakened by a lengthy period on short rations. Louse infestation was common, together with a shortage of water. More permanent P.O.W. camps in Italy and Germany were sometimes purpose-built stone barracks, or may previously have been a school or a castle. The camp at Eichstätt, *Oflag* VIIB, was previously a cavalry barracks, and that at Gavi, an old castle. Gavi was extremely damp and unpleasant in the winter. Here, officers slept eight or ten to a room 20 feet long by 12 feet wide, with one small window and one faint electric light. It was short of latrines and water. And there was no exercise space except the castle yard at restricted times. On the other hand, *Oflag* VIIB had fine grounds with garden, sports field, and two tennis

4

ourts for the use of prisoners. here were also parole walks the Bavarian countryside, and winter an ice-skating rink was epared.

Some of the worst conditions Europe were at the camp *flag* VIB at Dössel. In a desolate d exposed area, it comprised a umber of old wooden huts with aking roofs and walls. There ere no proper paths and the rea became a slough of mud hen it rained. The huts were t-infested, and beds and bed-ng were dirty and flea-ridden. etween 16 and 52 officers were uartered in rooms measuring feet by 12 feet. Latrines here scharged into three open cess-ools which, in bad weather, verflowed inside the camp.

Most prisoners experienced mething like this at some time their captivity. Many camps in

Europe were improved as time went on, and many of the improvements were due to the visits by neutrals.

Conditions did not improve in the Far East. Prisoners of the Japanese were imprisoned in various camps around Changi when they surrendered in early 1942. For the first few months, life was not intolerable, but conditions got worse as time went on. Five or six men were crammed in a one-man cell, rations were cut and drug supplies dwindled. The Japanese came to look on the prisoners only as a source of labour, and many of them were moved out of Changi to go to work in Borneo, where only a few survived the notorious death march, to go to Thailand to build the railway, or to go to Japan to work in the mines.

Conditions were really appalling at the jungle camps for the railway workers. The Japanese had a deadline to meet, and were not worried when their prisoners died in their hundreds from overwork, undernourishment, cholera, or malaria. To the Japanese, there were plenty more prisoners. The P.O.W.s lived in bamboo huts at these jungle camps, and monsoon rains added further to their discomfort. All except the officers were accustomed to being beaten up by Japanese guards, and men were

8. *An interesting contrast in expressions between a German Luftwaffe officer P.O.W. and his British Intelligence Corps sergeant escort.*
9. *German P.O.W.s on agricultural work in England.*
10. *May 19, 1945: the war in Europe is over, but not for these German prisoners. After being collected at a reception camp, they are being marched off to the station in batches of 50, under armed guard.*
11. *In Russia, huge columns of Axis P.O.W.s were frequently paraded through towns behind the front to show off the success of Soviet arms. From there the road led to P.O.W. camps and the most appalling conditions.*
12. *Many thousands of German prisoners gathered together at a concentration point outside Moscow.*
13. *German prisoners receive their food ration in a Russian camp.*
14. *Soup distribution in a Russian camp.*

14

15. Four Germans abandon the "Crusade against Bolshevism".

16. The "masters of the East" humbled. Ahead lay many years in the Russian camps unless they recanted their belief in the Nazi doctrine and admitted the superiority of the Soviet way of life.

17. The long wait for transport to a camp.

18. The other side of the coin: Poles, the first P.O.W.s of the war, receive their rations from the Germans.

sometimes beaten to death.

It is now well known how much the ill-treatment of P.O.W.s in the Far East owed to the Japanese tradition that a captive brought dishonour on himself and his family. In fact the traditions of the Imperial Japanese Army established a principle that the military honour of a soldier forbade his surrender to the enemy. The military regulations promulgated by the Japanese Minister of War in January 1942 reaffirmed the idea and made it enforceable. The Japanese training manual said "Those becoming prisoners-of-war will suffer the death penalty." Combat instructions advised troops to commit suicide rather than be captured. When a Japanese soldier left his family to join a combatant unit, a farewell ceremony was held in accordance with funeral rites;

and after his departure, he was regarded as dead by his family unless he should return as a conqueror. Since notification of his capture would disgrace his family, few Japanese desired it.

In view of these considerations, the attitude of Japanese troops towards their captives was hardly likely to be other than one of contempt. Since prisoners were little better than dead men, their living conditions were of small importance. It was no wonder that the Japanese authorities took little interest in transmitting information concerning captives. Their neglect of wounded prisoners and their murder of some of them were the logical consequences of their military code. The beatings into unconsciousness, the mass punishments in the presence of an arch-offender before his more frightful

19

19. *British prisoners and some of their Italian guards in the camp at San Bernardino in the sunny spring of 1945.*
20. *San Bernardino camp again, photographed by an Italian civilian.*
21. *Cheerful British prisoners from the sick-bay of* Stalag 357, *liberated by the British 7th Armoured Division on April 16, 1945. The Germans had managed to march off some 7,000 P.O.W.s, however, leaving only 350 British and a few Allied prisoners to be freed on the 16th.*
22. *British prisoners in* Oflag 79, *a camp for officers near Braunschweig (Brunswick).*
23. *San Bernardino camp.*

20

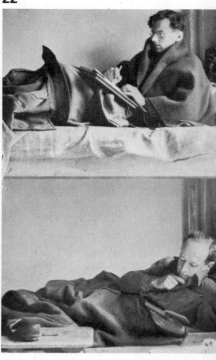

torture in private, the bayonet-ting to death and the beheading of recaptured escapers, all become more explicable in terms of the severe discipline of the Japanese.

The Nazi Government was committed to being *korrekt* in its observance of the Geneva Convention, and did not physically mistreat prisoners as did the Japanese, although they did shackle some British P.O.W.s at *Stalag* VIIIB, at *Stalag* IXC, and at Hehenfels. This was a High Command order and was a reprisal for British ill-treatment of German prisoners at the time of the Dieppe raid and also during the commando raid on Sark. As time went by, however, conditions were relaxed for the shackled prisoners.

It was also Nazi policy to use their prisoners to the utmost and make them as little of a drain on the national economy as possible. Officers and N.C.O.s did not have to work, but as many troops as could be were pushed out into farm work, coal-mining, factory work, and any unskilled tasks that would free Germans for a more active part in the war effort. Work camps were called *Arbeitskommandos*. The majority of them were in industrial areas, and sometimes in the centre of a town. Although long hours may have been expected, treatment of P.O.W.s was often quite good.

Prisoners who remained inside P.O.W. camps soon organised their lives. In 1942 Changi camp organised itself into an establishment of battalions, regiments, brigades, and divisions, each with

24. *Allied prisoners wait to be let out of the cages as the U.S. 9th Army liberates the huge camp at Altengrabow on April 5, 1945. A local truce had been arranged to give the liberators safe passage to and from the camp, which was some 15 miles behind the German lines. The camp held about 18,000 prisoners, including 1,500 Americans and 800 British, plus contingents from the French, Dutch, and Belgian forces.*
25. *After the liberation of Oflag 79, with its 1,957 officers and 412 other ranks: Private Walter Shaddick, who had been a prisoner in both World Wars, shows other ex-prisoners the can in which he kept potato peelings for hard times.*
26. *A small celebration as Oflag 79 is liberated: Inter-Keystone correspondent F. Ramage shakes hands with Lieutenant W. Vanderson, a British official photographer who had been a prisoner for 1,027 days.*
27. *Altogether grimmer—the camp run by the Japanese in Rangoon. These are men freed from the camp when the British arrived in May 1945.*
28. *A British prisoner, reduced to a travesty of his former self by his ordeal in a Japanese camp.*
29. *Recognition for those who did not last until the liberation in 1945: an ex-prisoner paints crosses for some of the 800 who died in the Singapore camp.*

25

26

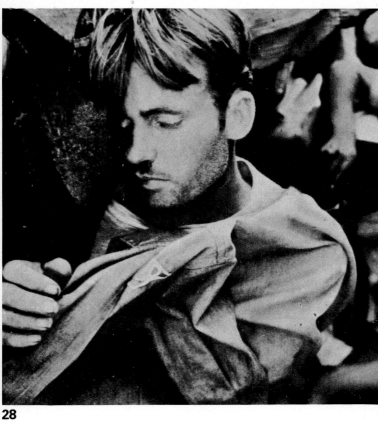

its own headquarters and formal staff. The digging of more bore-holes was organised to try to stem the dysentery outbreak, and the cook houses were adapted to meet the needs of such a vast influx of people. The Japanese gave food and money only to those who worked, so food was shared and each pay-day, workers made a contribution to a welfare fund which bought drugs and special foods for the sick.

The majority of P.O.W.s in camps in Europe had long periods during which conditions were bearable and when they made good use of their time. With amazing improvisation for which captivity was the stimulus, many were able to lead a vigorous and intellectual life. By summer 1942, for example, prisoners had got life at Lamsdorf pretty well organised. Enough supplies of Red Cross food, and private clothing and tobacco parcels arrived regularly. The medical supplies were adequate. Here, half a barrack was set aside as a

church, the other half serving as the camp school. There were vegetable and flower gardens and facilities for football, cricket, and all-in wrestling.

All these other activities did not prevent much attention being devoted to escaping. There were many attempts, both from permanent and work camps. Men tried to walk out of camps disguised in German uniforms, or tried to leave hidden in some form of transport. There was much tunnelling activity. Many camps had escape organisations, with escape officers. Here, all escape activity was co-ordinated, with the officers taking turns to warn of the approach of the German guards. These "escape routes", permitted many men to reach Allied territory. A series of mass breakouts in 1944 culminated in that from *Stalag Luft* III in March 1944, when 76 P.O.W.s escaped through tunnels. Three reached England, a few got to Danzig, but the majority were recaptured. Fifty of these were shot in the

back by the Gestapo.

Escape activity was different in the Far East. For white prisoners, there was the difficulty of conceal-ment in a city of Asiatics. Also, at Japanese camps, successful breakouts were followed by re-prisals on the rest of the inmates, and the knowledge of this did much to discourage attempts.

Medical treatment for P.O.W.s in Europe was not a great problem. The Red Cross was usually able to supply necessary medicines, and Allied prisoners were treated in German civil or military hospitals, or in special hospitals for P.O.W.s. There was no such treatment for prisoners in Japanese hands. No drugs reached them in usable quantities until the end of 1944, and under the appalling conditions already described, the medical teams had to rely on their own resources and initiative. Wood saws were used to amputate limbs, razor blades served as scalpels, and old pieces of clothing were the only available material for bandages.

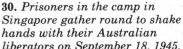

30. *Prisoners in the camp in Singapore gather round to shake hands with their Australian liberators on September 18, 1945.*

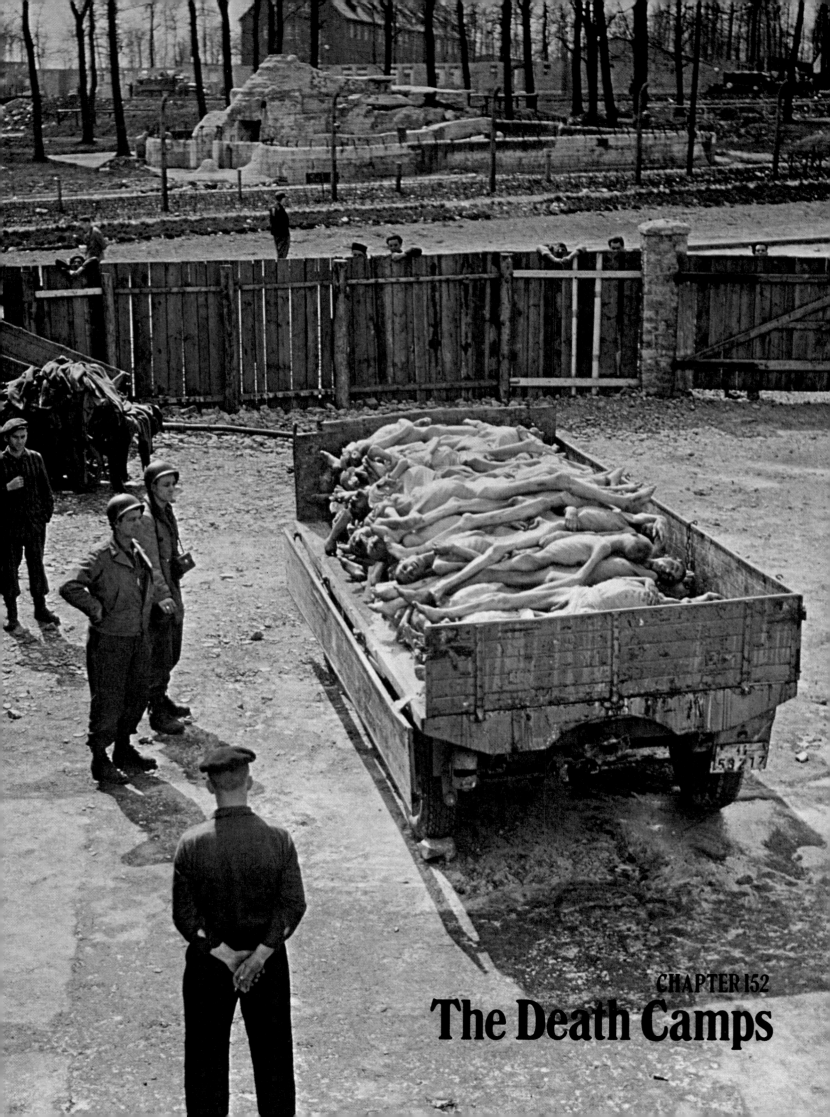

CHAPTER 152
The Death Camps

Previous page: *Previous page: The final appalling stages of the concentration camp system – American troops with the bodies of some of the last victims of Buchenwald camp, where some 63,500 prisoners died or were killed.*

△ *The early days: a batch of political prisoners, newly-arrived in Sachsenhausen, before changing their civilian clothes for camp uniforms.*

The Nazi concentration camp system was the most far-reaching and closely-concerted act of terror organised and carried out after January 30, 1933 by a state under the cover of legality. The terror itself was an expression of the huge breakdown of German society, of the inter-class struggle, and of the historical impasse of the 1930's. This impasse was not specifically German: it was world-wide, and because it was world-wide it made the German situation open-ended. That society's foundations were crumbling was evident from the world's increasingly rapid descent into war and from the almost simultaneous appearance of two concentration camp systems: the Soviet and the Nazi, each fed and controlled by state terror. In this wide setting the concentration camp takes on its full historical meaning: for the first time in modern history there is a very real, as opposed to an imaginary, possibility of a halt in human evolution, of humanity slipping down into organised barbarism.

The salient fact that the Nazi counter-revolution developed not before the seizure of power by the party, but after the legal installation of this power and on the legal basis of the state, plays a very important part in the development of the concentration camp system, determining its administration, its function, and its régime. Its basic function was to carry to its conclusion the state's policy of political and social violence, and it was in the very accomplishment of this task, in the thoroughness with which it was carried out, that the concentration camp somehow emancipated itself from the state which created it, becoming a social force within itself, then, by its own internal growth, profoundly altering the entire network of social relationships.

The political prisoner was to be the typical concentration camp detainee, and by political prisoner must be meant all those who, by their ideas and convictions, represented a resistance, active or passive, suspected or real, against one or the other of the activities of the establishment. He could be a communist, a socialist, a liberal, or a democrat, a trades unionist or a member of a university, a Christian, a pacifist, or merely a fanatic. They all, from the state's point of view, represented evil. Opposition was not considered as opposition but as a crime, and disagreement as heresy. This idea of evil brought in the irrationality of unbridled passions, and once society began to break down, it became irrational in all its activities, but retained an inner logic which dominated the concentration camp world.

The aim of the concentration camp was not just the death of the guilty, but a slow death by degradation. From the Nazi point of view that was one of the basic differences between the treatment of the political prisoner and the treatment of the Jew. The political prisoner was the subjective evil, conscious of himself. The Jew was the objective evil, like a poisonous plant. The plant had to be plucked out, the Jew destroyed. The problem of the destruction of the Jew was a mass problem which was to pose acute logistical questions of means and time. The humiliations the Jews were made to suffer were in the order of personal satisfaction for the oppressors. At the level of general directives, it was a question only of humiliation.

The political prisoner, on the other hand, had to be punished. The supreme punishment was to be the gradual destruction of his humanity. Death was the end, certainly, but death must be expected and prepared for in suffering. This function of the camp was so basic that it was to remain even when the necessities of war and the personal interests of the S.S. made concentration camp prisoners into a labour force, and the camps became part of the production process. Suffering was always to have priority over production.

The death of the political prisoner demanded time, therefore – a time filled with suffering, and a time for the camps to develop into societies.

The war was to bring most of Europe into this universe.

▽ *Roll-call at the Sachsenhausen camp near Berlin in February 1941. During the course of the war some 100,000 prisoners died here.*
▽▽ *Punishment parade in Sachsenhausen: the roll had been called three times to establish that a prisoner had escaped, and then the commandant ordered that the rest of the prisoners stand on parade ground in ten degrees of frost until the missing prisoner was found.*

△ *The beginning of the mass extermination of the Jews: German troops start to round up Polish Jews for transport to the camps.*

△▷ *Humiliation as well as the threat of death: a Jewish woman, stripped and beaten by the Nazis when they entered L'vov on June 29, 1941, tries in vain to cover her nakedness.*

▷ *A Jewess forced to strip by the Nazis of L'vov.*

The system spreads

At 0600 hours on March 15, 1939, German tanks rolled into Bohemia. That same evening Hitler made a thunderous entry into Prague. "Czechoslovakia has ceased to exist." Himmler appointed Dr. Hans Frank Chief of Police of the Protectorate. On September 1, 1939 German tanks drove into the heart of Poland. On October 7 Hitler appointed *Reichsführer*-S.S. Heinrich Himmler head of a new organisation: the Reich Commissariat for the Strengthening of the German Nation (R.K.F.D.V.). Poles and Jews were to be deported from the annexed Polish provinces and replaced by Germans. On October 9 Himmler decreed that 550,000 out of the 650,000 Jews from these pro-

vinces were to be sent east of the Vistula. In one year, in fact, 1,200,000 Poles and 300,000 Jews were to disappear to the East.

The hour for mighty tasks had struck. For the first time the formidable Nazi terror apparatus had a real job to do: mass extermination. On August 22, on the eve of the Polish operation, Hitler is reported to have said, in a somewhat oracular tone, to his generals assembled at Obersalzberg, that certain things were to happen which would not be to their liking and that they were warned not to meddle. On October 18 General Halder noted in his diary a conversation Hitler had had that day with the Quartermaster General, Eduard Wagner, who reported it to him:

"The Polish intelligentsia must be prevented from rising to become a ruling class. Life must be preserved at a low level only. Cheap slaves."

Frank was appointed Governor General of Poland with a first task of eliminating the Polish intellectuals, which his directives called an "extraordinary action of pacification". It would be of no avail to seek an explanation of this policy in Hitler's psychological make-up or in the dementia characteristic of the S.S. The orders carried out were the exact replicas of Stalin's in the Baltic states and against various other national minorities.

It was therefore a general phenomenon characteristic of this period, the origins of which are to be sought in the breakdown of world society, in the spread of state-organised terror in the two countries concerned, and in the deep disturbances caused in every field of activity by the growth of the concentration camp system. Terror created the camps which, as they developed, increased the impact of the acts of terror, which in turn gave further impetus to the camp system. In the Nazi case, the phenomenon is clearly seen in its spatial development and its social effects. Each stage brought a spectacular increase in S.S. bureaucracy and a growth of its powers, so that its importance to the state increased continually and caused typical distortions of the social framework at all levels.

The suppression of the intelligentsia was no act of folly. It showed an exact understanding of modern society and its level of development. It is undeniable that the physical annihilation of the whole of the intellectual class stops social growth immediately and then leads to its rapid regression. That such a strategy can have been put into practice reveals in the most striking way the depth of barbarism of which Hitler and Stalin were the active agents. What their henchmen did not understand was that inevitably these acts were to produce a similar regression amongst themselves. The logic of terror is stronger than those who unleash it. The annihilation in Poland was to spread to Russia. The destruction of the Jews was thus only one particular case in an overall policy. Yet it is a truly extraordinary case which seems to be an exclusive product of Nazism. Nothing shows more clearly the extent to which certain circles were haunted by the Jewish question than this letter from General von Fritsch to his friend the Baroness Margot von Schutzbar in December 1938. The general hated Himmler and the S.S. By the meanest of provocations they nearly cost him his

honour. They broke his career. Yet he could write: "Shortly after the War I became convinced that we would have to win three victories if we were to recover our power:

1. Against the working classes. Hitler has won this one.
2. Against the Catholic Church, or rather against the Ultramontanes.
3. Against the Jews.

"We're in the middle of the last two, and that against the Jew is the more difficult."

It was difficult because of the large numbers of Jews involved when the S.S. had to tackle it on a European scale and wipe them out. At the Nuremberg trials a

▷ One of the crematoria in the extermination camp at Maidanek, where at least 1,380,000 people were murdered by the Nazis. After being gassed, the bodies of the victims were taken down to the ovens and burned, the ashes then being crumbled, so easing the problem of disposal.
▽ Ovens in the "model" camp at Terezín in Czechoslovakia, which could take 190 corpses at a time.
▷▷ The human incinerator in the camp at Gardelegen, about 40 miles north-east of Braunschweig.
▽▷ A Polish woman weeps over the remains of some of those murdered at Maidanek.
▽▷▷ Even in death the victims of Nazi tyranny served a purpose, even if only by providing spectacles for reclamation.

△ *The grisly remains of some of Maidanek's many thousands of innocent victims.*

directive addressed to Heydrich by Göring was produced. It was dated July 31, 1941, and expressly said: "This is to give you full powers to make preparations concerning a total solution of the Jewish question in the European territories under German control."

Heydrich was to say before 15 high-ranking civil servants on June 20, 1942: "The Final Solution of the Jewish problem in Europe affects approximately 11 million Jews." He then explained how they were to be concentrated in the East and employed on the hardest work. "The rest," he went on, "those who survive (and they will doubtless be the toughest), will have to be treated, for in them we shall have, by a process of natural selection, the germ of a new Jewish expansion."

On February 21, 1940, S.S. *Brigadeführer* Richard Glücks, head of the Concentration Camp Inspectorate, wrote to Himmler to say that he had found a suitable site near Auschwitz, a little town of some 12,000 inhabitants, lost in the marshes, with some old barrack buildings formerly belonging to the Austrian cavalry. On June 14 Auschwitz got its first Polish political detainees, who were to be treated harshly. At the same time I. G. Farben decided to establish at Auschwitz a synthetic petrol and rubber plant. In the spring of 1940 the S.S. arrived with, at their head, two of the greatest criminals in the Nazi concentration camp world: Josef Kramer and Rudolf Franz Hoess. The latter stated with some satisfaction at Nuremberg that he had presided over the extermination of 2,500,000 people at Auschwitz, not including, he added, another half million who had had the right to starve to death.

Thus the Auschwitz zone, the most extensive and the most sinister, came into being. Then there appeared the mass extermination camps, the *Vernichtungslager*. The organisation of the vast complex of Auschwitz was exactly like that of all other concentration camp towns, surrounded by their satellites. The gas chambers introduced one more degree of terror.

Insuperable organisational problems

In their immediate, least refined, but most military objective, general terror methods aimed at annihilation raise problems of mass and speed which are difficult to solve. In 1939 Himmler and Heidrich decided in principle on the setting up of "Special Action Groups" or *Einsatzgruppen,* with four units labelled A, B, C, and D. They were to follow the troops advancing into Poland and later into Russia. Their objective would be the elimination of political commissars and Jews. They solved two minor problems: keeping the army out of it and giving the S.S. an autonomous military body, adapted to its purpose and therefore efficient. One of the leaders, Otto Ohlendorf, formerly head of *Amt* III of the Central Office of Reich Security *(Reichssicherheitshauptamt* or R.S.H.A.) then, from June 1941 to June 1942, of *Einsatzgruppe* D attached to the 2nd Army in the south Ukraine, declared at Nuremberg that his men had executed 90,000 men, women, and children. In a report seized later by the Allies, *Gruppe* A, operating in Belorussia and the Baltic states, estimated that it killed 229,052 Jews up to January 31, 1942. According to Eichmann, the *Einsatzgruppen* working in the East exterminated two million people, most of them Jews. Efficient though the special groups were in certain respects, their work could not be secret and, given the size of their task, was low in productivity.

In the spring of 1942 Himmler authorised the introduction of "gas vans" especially for the extermination of women and children. Ohlendorf explained how they worked: "You could not guess their purpose from their outside appearance," he said. "They were like closed lorries and were built so that when the engine started the exhaust fumes filled the inside, causing death in 10 to 15 minutes."

These were a step forward in the matter of secrecy, but they did not add much to the speed of the operation. There were not enough of them. Their use also brought dangerous psychological consequences on those who worked them. Even for the specialised troops it took some nerve to bring out all the bodies. The worst was that they only killed 15 to 25 at a time. The real progress came with the installation of gas chambers in Auschwitz. These meant secrecy, speed, and no psychological consequences. The loneliness of the site ensured total secrecy. The time was cut to three to 15 minutes. Quantity was satisfactory: in the last period a gas chamber at Birkenau could kill 6,000 people a day. The psychological consequences were eliminated as the bodies were handled by a *Sonderkommando,* detainees who would themselves be exterminated a few months later. When the system was fully operative, however, there were bottlenecks in the transfer of the bodies from the chambers to the cremation ovens. In spite of several

▽ *The "refuse" of murder in Maidanek.*
▽▽ *Charred corpses in a mass grave.*

Ilse Förster   *Georg Krafft*   *Klara Oppitz*   *Kurt Sendsitzky*   *Martha Linke*   *Walter Otto*

suggestions no workable solution was found.

The setting-up of this procedure was clearly explained by Rudolf Hoess in his evidence. "In June 1941," he said, "I received the order to organise the extermination at Auschwitz. I went to Treblinka to see how it operated there. The commandant at Treblinka told me that he had got rid of 80,000 detainees in six months... He used carbon monoxide...

"But his methods did not seem very efficient to me. So when I set up the extermination block at Auschwitz I chose *Zyklon* B, crystallised prussic acid which we dropped into the death cells through a little hole. It took from 3 to 15 minutes according to atmospheric conditions for the gas to have effect. We also improved on Treblinka by building gas chambers holding 2,000, whereas theirs only held 200."

A Nuremberg witness spoke of the duties of the *Sonderkommando:* "The first job was to get rid of the blood and the excrement before separating the interlocked bodies which we did with hooks and nooses, before we began the horrible search for gold and the removal of hair and teeth, which the Germans considered strategic raw materials. Then the bodies were sent up by lifts or in waggons on rails to the ovens, after which the remains were crushed to a fine powder."

The gas chamber method at Auschwitz gave rise to a further refinement: selection. The detainees were selected on first arriving, then again more or less periodically within the camp and this caused an extraordinary increase in terror.

On July 22, 1941, Keitel signed two directives: "In view of the considerable extent of the area of occupation in Soviet territory," the first one ran, "the security of the German armed forces can only be assured if all resistance on the part of the civilian population is punished, not by the legal prosecution of the guilty, but by measures of terror which are the only ones which can efficiently strangle all inclination to rebel." In the second directive Keitel laid on Himmler the "special duty" of drawing up plans for the administration of Russia. To achieve this Hitler specified that he had delegated to Himmler the right to act on his own responsibility and with absolute power. Keitel then made clear the Führer's intentions by decreeing that the "occupied zones will be out of bounds during the time Himmler is carrying out his operations." No one was to be admitted, not even the highest-ranking party officials.

The concentration camp system was now in full swing. It was the basis of the social and political dominance of the S.S. The power of the S.S. was practically at its height. In the very middle of the war it was still stronger than the army. It dominated the party. It had a stranglehold on the administration. It was going to reach the peak of its power by bringing the concentration camps into the production lines.

Change of emphasis

1942 was the great turning point, the year in which the concentration camp was integrated in the production process. This was brought about by four fundamental documents:

An ordinance of March 1942 transferred the administration of the camps (*Konzentrationslager* or K.Z.) from the Central Office of Reich Security (R.S.H.A.) to the economic and administrative services of the S.S., the S.S. *Wirtschaftsverwaltungshauptamt* (W.V.H.A.), directed by S.S. *Obergruppenführer* and *General des Waffen*-S.S. Oswald Pohl.

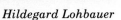

Hildegard Lohbauer   *Franz Horich*   *Gertrude Faist*   *Peter Weingartner*   *Elisabeth Volkenrath*   *Wladislaw Ostrewski*

In an ordinance dated March 3 and enabling documents of April 30, Pohl set up the Concentration Camp Work Charter. The aims state: "The war has clearly changed the structure of the K.Z. and our task as far as detention is concerned. The imprisonment of detainees for sole reasons of security, correction, or prevention, is not the first object. The importance has now shifted to the field of the economy . . . This has caused certain measures to be taken which will allow the K.Z. to progress from their former purely political rôle to organisations adapted to economic tasks."

The charter had as its prime objective to "insert in the new course of events the essential and permanent function of the concentration camps as conceiving work as a means of punishment and extermination." The constraints were therefore increased, and this is the clearest difference between a concentration camp worker and a slave.

Articles 4, 5, and 6 made decisive provisions and revealed without any doubt the real spirit behind the undertaking:

"Article 4: the Camp Commandant alone is responsible for the use to which the workers are put. This can be exhausting (erschöpfend) in the literal sense so as to achieve the highest productivity.

"Article 5: length of work to be limitless . . . to be laid down by the Commandant alone.

"Article 6: anything which can shorten work (meal-times, roll-calls, etc.) to be reduced to the strict minimum. Movements and mid-day breaks for rest alone are forbidden."

In his comments, Pohl added that the detainees were to be "fed, accommodated, and treated in a way such as to obtain the maximum out of them with the minimum cost."

The articles are of salient interest. They are the legal basis of the S.S. ownership of the concentration camp labour force. They define the system of extermination by work: "The S.S. Commandant alone is responsible for the use to which the workers are put." Therefore the worker did not belong to the state, that is to the Minister of Labour, or of Armaments, or of War Production, and he could not be handed over by the state to private enterprise. So that the state could use him, so that a private firm could employ him, an agreement had to be reached with and a fee paid to the S.S., which, with its autonomous bureaucracy, was the sole owner of the concentration camp worker. This gave it an economic monopoly. Thus the S.S. became rooted in the production process.

"The S.S. Commandant alone is responsible for the system of work." The S.S. was thus in law the owner not only of the work force but also of the worker's whole person without restriction of any kind. This provision gave the S.S. the authority and the means to carry out its job of extermination. Minister of Justice Thierack, describing a conversation he had just had with Goebbels, explained the word *erschöpfend*. To define the new régime he used the expression "extermination through work" (*Vernichtung durch Arbeit*). Hoess reported to the Nuremberg trial: *"Obergruppenführer* Pohl told a meeting of camp leaders that every detainee must be used up to the last ounce of his strength for the armament industry." It was Pohl also who defined for the Nuremberg jury the "Final Solution of the Jewish question" as "the extermination of Jewry".

On September 18 an agreement was reached between Himmler and Thierack on the transfer of Jews, social drop-outs, Hungarian gypsies, Russians, Ukrainians, etc. from prisons to concentration camps with a view to their "extermination through work".

△ *Guards at the Bergen-Belsen concentration camp, to which sick prisoners from other camps were sent for "recuperation". A total of about 50,000 people died here.*

These texts were preceded and prepared by a series of decisions. The decision in principle to turn the detainees into a labour force was taken on June 23, 1939, by the Council for the Defence of the Reich. Dr. Funk, Economics Minister, got the job of deciding "the work to be given to the prisoners of war and the concentration camp detainees". Himmler intervened and said: "Concentration camps will be drawn on more extensively in war-time." Yet it was not until September 29, 1941, that a first application was made, and this was only preparatory: a directive from the Inspector of Camps recommending the setting up in each camp of an *Arbeitseinsatz* service, i.e. to administer labour. A first indication of the turning-point was on November 15 when, correcting an order dated November 9 by the head of the Gestapo, Heinrich Müller, Himmler made it known that Red Army political commissars sent to the K.Z. for execution could be employed in quarries (work considered, and rightly so, as particularly hard).

These basic texts were followed by a set of executive measures, the first and most widely applicable being the ordinance of December 14, 1942, under which the numbers interned in the camps were to be increased by 35,000 able bodied detainees. The ordinance was sent to all police services on December 17. On March 23 Kaltenbrunner, who took over from Heydrich as head of the R.S.H.A., ordered this plan to be carried out.

Turning point

It is clear from Himmler's explanations to the S.S. at Poznań in 1943 that a turning point was reached with the "extermination through work" plan, and that those concerned knew it very well. Recalling 1941 (and nothing shows more clearly that until then the 1939 decision of principle had not yet been put into effect) he said: "We didn't look on this mass of humanity then in the same light as we do now: a brutish mass, a labour force. We deplore, not as a generation but as a potential work force, the loss of prisoners by the million from exhaustion and starvation." Let no one be deceived. Himmler and the S.S. had not been converted to economics.

The usual plundering of Jews' property was a by-product, not a cause, of their

deportation. Göring was able to claim: "I received a letter written by Bormann on orders from the Führer requiring a co-ordinated approach to the Jewish question. As the problem was primarily an economic one, it had to be tackled from the economic point of view." He was preaching to the wind. Selection was to go on as in the past. No examination was made of a detainee's real qualifications or state of health. Selection on arrival and inside the camps was still an act of terror. A potentially very powerful labour force continued to be sacrificed

◁ *"In Auschwitz" by H. Olomucka.*
△ △ *Female guards unload bodies from a waggon into a mass grave at Belsen.*
△ *Dead in Auschwitz.*

to the vengeance of the S.S.

The supreme criterion was still the disintegration of human beings, their abasement, and their slow death, however. Whatever the importance of this turning point, it did not affect the essential function of the camps. It merely gave them a different emphasis. The real, the crucial discovery was that through a concentration camp labour-force two key objectives were reached: production was maintained, and punishment meted out.

The second major discovery was that the labour force increased the power of the S.S. so much that it transformed it. However, right to the very end, the norms of destruction were more important than those of productivity: those who survived the camps know this well. This comes out of the statutory instruments so clearly

that these can show the difference in law between slave labour and concentration camp labour. The slave- or serf-owner took elementary precautions in his own interests, and in the interests of production, to keep the labour force alive. The concentration camp saw to it that everything was done to exterminate the labour force by wearing it out. If economic sense and logic were to prevail, this would clearly be aberrant. This constant will to destroy had one far-reaching consequence: the need for a rapid renewal of the work force. All legal decisions became null and void in the face of this need. The slightest accusation, well-founded or not, the most commonplace of court sentences could open the gates of the camps when there were numbers to make up. People would be hounded down

▽ *The ovens of Buchenwald.*

by terror more than ever. Yet these swoops by the secret police had their fixed basic rules. Transport difficulties were so appalling that the losses in transit were enormous. The pressure of events was relentless.

The cause of the turning point lay completely in the unexpected prolongation of the war, in the great extent of the front, in the continuation, in spite of everything, of Blitzkrieg strategy, and in the effects of all this on manpower and industry. It was in the winter of 1941-42 that Field-Marshal Wilhelm Keitel raised the whole vital question of manpower. The army needed an annual reserve of two to two and a half million men. Normal recruitment, plus the return of the wounded and some barrel-scraping, could produce only one million. This left a million and a half to be found elsewhere. "Elsewhere" could only mean on the production lines. Factories had therefore to work at full capacity and beyond it to meet the ever-increasing needs and to make up for the now dangerous contribution to the Allied effort from the United States. So the whole of Europe had to be mobilised, and this could only be done by intensifying constraints and terror.

The general staff of the forced-labour administration consisted of Keitel, Speer, Sauckel, and Himmler. Keitel was responsible for the recruitment of army, navy, and air force reserves. Albert Speer ran the Todt Organisation from February 15, 1942, and was then put in charge of

what, on September 2, 1943, became the Ministry of Armament and War Production. Fritz Sauckel, nominated General Plenipotentiary for the Allocation of Labour, had the job of putting into effect the forced labour programme. Finally Himmler was the number one contractor.

This very considerable undertaking brought a clash between two branches of state service under Keitel and Speer on the one hand and Himmler on the other. Keitel represented military bureaucracy and Speer the joint interests of the state and powerful private enterprise, and his was a key ministry, as it brought monopolies into the state system. High-ranking management jobs were given to industrialists who at the same time remained in charge of their firms. Sauckel was merely an executive. Speer indicated to him what was wanted, Himmler provided the means. Sauckel co-ordinated. In January 1944, when Hitler ordered Sauckel to recruit four million workers, Himmler replied that to get them he would increase the number of concentration camp detainees and make them all work harder.

The matter which brought Keitel and Speer up against Himmler was the key question of who owned the forced labour gangs, and in particular the concentration camp labourers. Keitel and Speer said the state, which had sovereign rights over them. Himmler replied the S.S., and to employ them there had to be a contract with his economic service or, more

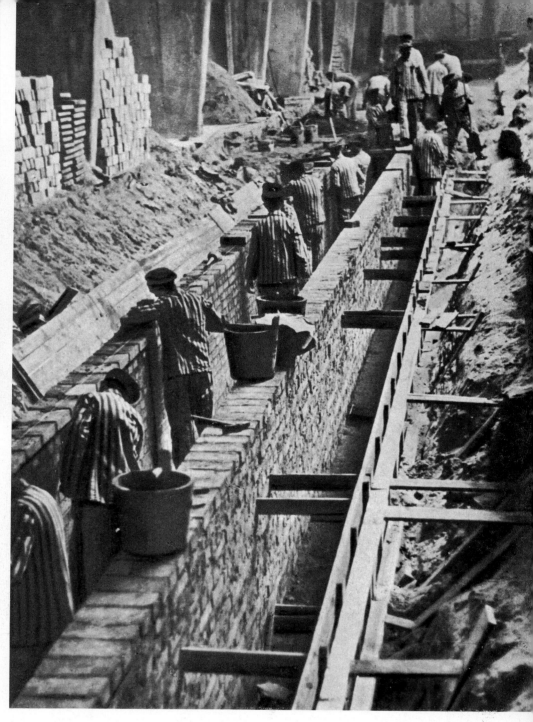

precisely, with his *Amtsgruppe* D, which ran the camps, or with the K.Z. commandants who, under the Pohl ordinance, had sole control of the use of the camp labour force. Fundamentally what was at stake was the ownership of the slave and concentration camp labour and the position of all hostile elements in production and society. At Nuremberg Keitel revealed Himmler's empire-building, his constant efforts to bring under his control prisoners-of-war, and then foreign and requisitioned workers.

In September 1942 Hitler was called upon to settle the differences between the two totally opposed sides. Speer proposed that private enterprise should take over the camp detainees. His main argument was that this was the only way to get high productivity. Himmler retorted that industries should be set up inside the camps, as only the S.S. were legally qualified to deal jointly with the needs of production and repression. Speer objected that this could not be done because of the shortage of machine tools. Himmler agreed to a compromise: some industries to be set up in the camps and some camps to be organised around existing industries. Factories would be built in regions where there were large concentration camp complexes. The ownership of the concentration camp labour force was recognised as belonging in law and in fact to the S.S. Private management and monopolies were required to pay to the S.S. a fee for each prisoner employed for the whole time he worked for them.

▷ *Germany was short not only of manpower, but also of fuel and draught animals, as these men from Sachsenhausen camp harnessed to a waggon bear witness.*
▽ *Some of the hardest work of all for debilitated prisoners: quarrying.*

Moreover, Speer had to agree to turn over to the S.S. five per cent of all the arms made by the detainees. A conflict of principles was to become a conflict of execution. Himmler got his way then, because he was indispensable. To get the workers they needed, Keitel, Speer, and Sauckel had to use the S.S. and its terror methods. They may have disliked it but they could not do without it. The logic of the system worked for the S.S.

Behind all this there were totally opposed ideas. For Speer the decisive criterion was productivity. For the Party and the S.S. it was terror, as a social function. Speer won the concession, *against the Party,* that Jews could work in arms factories. *On Hitler's order* they were to be excluded in 1943 and *in spite of this order* 100,000 Hungarian Jews were to work in underground factories in 1943. This gives Göring's letter quoted above its true meaning.

The S.S. had made its final change and become an economic power. The importance of this was not that it achieved great wealth collectively by this change, but that it obtained the final means for its independence and established its stranglehold on the state.

The only by-product of extermination which brought in huge fortunes, the gold from the Jewish corpses at Auschwitz and the valuables taken from deportees, were deposited in the *Reichsbank,* where by an agreement between Dr. Walther Funk and Himmler they were credited to the S.S. in an account entered under the name of "Max Heiliger." The deposits came so quickly and in such large quantities that to clear the vaults the bankers went to pawnbrokers and turned them into cash.

Continued growth

When the S.S. came into the production processes there was a rapid spread of the concentration camp system throughout all German society. Firstly there was a direct effort. Concentration camp labour was used everywhere: first of all in the hardest and most secret work (digging out underground factories, making V-1's and V-2's), for which it was well qualified by its isolation, cheapness, limitless exploitability, and expendability; then for all hard work in the heavy, the precision, and the peripheral in-

dustries; and then in all categories as unskilled labourers, navvies, skilled workers, technicians, and so on.

Then there was the indirect method: by contamination. Dora and Ellrich were both centres of V-1 and V-2 production and for a long time the hell of Buchenwald. By the spring of 1944 mines were being extensively used as arms factories. In April 1944 work began on the *Schacht Marie* salt mine, and soon 2,000 women were employed on the machines there. In that same month Göring asked Himmler for the largest number of concentration camp workers possible. Himmler replied that already he had 36,000 working for the air force and would examine the possibility of raising this to 90,000. Concentration camp detainees worked in the

△ *Prisoners from Oranienburg, part of the Sachsenhausen complex in Brandenburg, operating a huge cement mixer during the building of a factory in Berlin.*

▷ *A scene from the propaganda film "The Führer Gives the Jews a New Town", showing how well the Nazis treated the Jews. In fact these are the vegetable plots of the guards at the model camp at Theresienstadt (Terezín), all cared for by prisoners detailed for the job.*
▽ *Emaciated prisoners freed by the Allies in 1945 from the main Austrian camp, Mauthausen, where 138,500 prisoners died.*

▷▷ *A Czech barber bids farewell to a friend, a Russian soldier murdered by a German guard in a labour camp.*
▽▷ *The ideal for which millions died: the safeguarding of a clean-cut Aryan future.*

building trade in Sachsenhausen, in the brick works at Klinker, on the Annaberg motorway; they drained the marshes at Ravensbrück and Auschwitz, dug canals at Wansleben, opened up roads at Küstrin, built a submarine base near Bremen, airfields in East Prussia, made spare parts for Messerschmitts, and assembled planes at Gusen II. Amongst the documents seized in the S.S.W.V.H.A. archives, one dated November 4, 1942, was a request for specialists from the head of *Amt* III at Oranienburg to the commandant of the Natzweiler camp. Thirty-one categories were asked for (accountants, welders, oxy-acetylene welders, mechanics etc.).

The S.S. certainly took care to register a detainee's real or pretended qualifications on his arrival. The detainees themselves looked after this even more actively. To get into a factory was a much sought-after privilege. It could mean the difference between life or death. The harshest treatment in a factory was paradise compared with navvying, quarrying or the hell of the S.S. and the cold.

The numbers of workers handled were very large and the overall organisation became unwieldy and inflexible. Old-fashioned procedures such as work-books led the administrative constraints. Besides the concentration camp workers, there were seven and a half million foreign workers and two million prisoners-of-war in Germany in September 1944. At Nuremberg, Sauckel confessed that only about 200,000 out of five million foreign workers were volunteers. Albert Speer admitted that 40 per cent of the prisoners-of-war in Germany were being employed on arms and munitions production or related work in 1944. These large numbers meant an automatic change in the organisation of labour.

It is difficult to establish the proportion of concentration camp workers in the whole of the forced labour gangs. Most of the records have disappeared, and where they do exist they were so much subject to the usual camouflage and falsification that they are difficult to interpret. Krupp stated during his trial that out of his 190,000 workers half were forced labour. It has been possible to find the distribution of the latter: there were 69,898 civilians from the East, 23,076 prisoners-of-war, and 4,897 concentration camp detainees. So one in 39 of the Krupp labour force came from the concentration camp, a striking figure.

▷ *Ravensbrück in north Germany, where 92,000 women prisoners died.*
▽ *Buchenwald camp.*
▷ ▷ *Buchenwald, main camp for the Brandenburg region.*
▽ ▷ *Ravensbrück, a camp exclusively for women. It is noteworthy how solidly these early camps were built. Only with the start of the war and later the "Final Solution" was it necessary to lower standards and build wooden or prefabricated camps.*

▷ *Prisoners freed in Auschwitz-Birkenau by the Russians in January 1945. In this worst camp of all, at least two million people lost their lives.*
▽ *Woman and child in Auschwitz.*

Striking though it may be, the figure does not reveal the true implications of the system. Terror created the K.Z., and the K.Z. reacted on the S.S. by increasing the field of action of terror. This increase reached frightful proportions once the K.Z./S.S. complex was integrated in the production process. The fundamental dynamism of society provided a feedback.

It is a quite remarkable sociological phenomenon that as soon as a certain critical density was achieved, the spread of the concentration camp ethos became automatic. There was nothing abstract about the phenomenon: experience showed it in its concrete form. It can be grasped in the rise of the conflict between private monopolies and the S.S. over the legal ownership of the labour force.

The simplest and best-tried rules of productivity ought to have led the private sector, once it took in concentration camp labour, to restore normal conditions of life for the workers (food, safety at work, rest, and hygiene). Far from it: the private monopolies strove on the contrary to adapt their regulations to those of the camps.

I.G. Farben invested 250 million dollars in factories in the Auschwitz area. The labour force of a few hundred thousand came from the two million detainees who passed through Auschwitz from 1941 to 1943. It sent 100,000 of them back to the gas chambers. It paid the S.S. a fee for every worker employed, and this was remitted when the worker died or was sent back to the camp because he could work no more.

The I.G. Farben administration, on the other hand, did concern itself with the worker as soon as he left the camp. Very

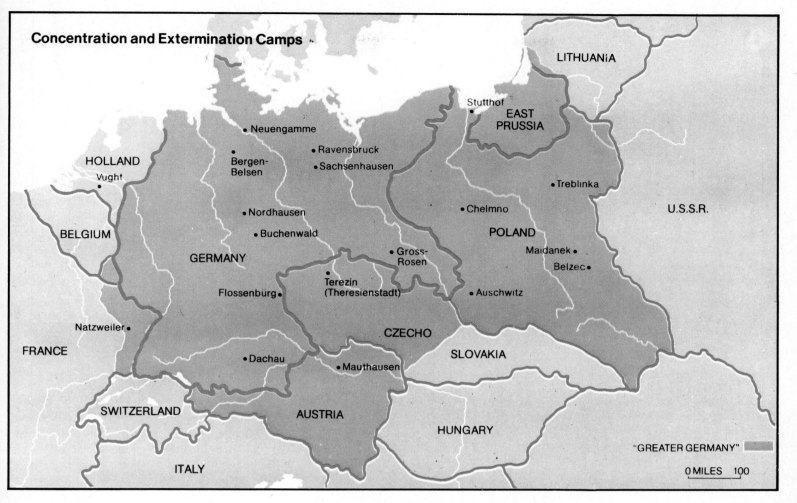

Concentration and Extermination Camps

Map labels:
LITHUANiA
Stutthof
EAST PRUSSIA
Neuengamme
Ravensbruck
HOLLAND
Bergen-Belsen
Sachsenhausen
Treblinka
Vught
U.S.S.R.
Nordhausen
Chelmno
BELGIUM
Buchenwald
POLAND
GERMANY
Maidanek
Gross-Rosen
Belzec
Flossenbürg
Terezin (Theresienstadt)
Auschwitz
Natzweiler
CZECHO
FRANCE
SLOVAKIA
Dachau
Mauthausen
SWITZERLAND
AUSTRIA
HUNGARY
ITALY
"GREATER GERMANY"
0 MILES 100

△ *The concentration camp system in "greater Germany" and occupied countries.*

carefully-kept records were found with entries showing a worker's behaviour, sickness, and death. The conflict between I.G. Farben and the S.S. may have been a quarrel over the amount of the fee to be paid, but it was really about the S.S.'s right to determine the kind of work and how it was to be checked. The S.S. had to be allowed into the factory: supervision of a man's work led inevitably to increased supervision of the factory itself. As the S.S. already had its own factories and workshops, as its influence on administration was enormous, and as it could act to affect all markets, to allow it to occupy a firm base inside the business itself was tantamount to giving it all up. And so I.G. stated that it would only hand back the camp worker to the S.S. either dead or dying and this the S.S. would not accept.

I.G. Farben therefore took the labour *Kommandos* in. It did not change the detainees' working conditions, but adapted its factory to meet these conditions. Towards the middle of 1942, the Buna rubber and chemicals factory was surrounded by barbed wire: the S.S. were forbidden to enter except for "very special reasons". The same thing at Monowitz,

a factory founded by I.G. Farben, now an I.G. Farben camp. This was allowed on the pretext that the daily journey to and from the concentration camp meant a loss of production. I.G. Farben therefore had to set up its own concentration camp management system. This it did on a system based on the S.S. model.

The way I.G. Farben ran its camp was identical to the K.Z. system. The S.S. actually denounced it as inhuman, saying that the mortality rate was too high – a tragic and derisory accusation. Buna (not including Leuna) had 300,000 concentration camp detainees, of whom 200,000 died. Out of the 20,000 deportees in Monowitz (which had been built to hold 5,000) 15,000 were sent to hospitals in 1943 and 10,000 "exterminated through work".

Krupp ran identical camps at Essen. They became a general feature in industrial areas and show how profoundly labour relations had changed. The process was there for all to see. The extension of the war forced Germany's leaders to seek a large and increasing number of foreign workers. Good wages and a decent standard of living were not possible. This meant a resort to force, and

force was possible because the régime was founded on terror. Bureaucracy, which had the monopoly of terror, seized its chance to extend its power in and over the state. As the legally-recognised owner of the person of the deportee, it sought to increase the numbers of people it controlled, and to control the total of forced labour workers and the reserve of free workers. This it could do only by increasing its interventions and supervision. By virtue of its right over the detainee, it built up its own economic interests and gained entry to the factory. When this activity had reached a certain level its constraints over the organisation of labour became automatic. From its hold over the labour force, it passed *de facto* and *de jure* to a hold over the person of the worker. The administrative constraints structured the production processes, and were in themselves only a projection of the concentration camp system. The apparatus of terror (the social *corpus* of terror), became free of state control. The S.S. bureaucracy thus tamed the state. Only defeat broke this development before it was complete.

Camp society

The inclusion of the camp detainees in the production process greatly affected society outside the camps: but it also transformed the camps internally, making

them into societies. It brought great changes in the camp administration and diversified it. It extended the camp network in a new and original way. It increased the differences between camps. It strengthened the rôle of the centres, that is of the concentration camp complexes. It increased the outside worker *Kommandos* which tended to take root. It operated sharp distinctions between detainees and these distinctions became clearly social. The differences became based on social classes. It increased outside contacts and created complex links with firms. It consequently widened the basis of corruption and noticeably increased the detainee bureaucracy's chances of manoeuvre. It brought a radical change to this bureaucracy. Ordinary criminals gave way to political detainees. This shift of power came about through unheard-of violence, by a series of plots and a large number of murders. It split the S.S. Once the political detainees got power, the history of the camps took a new course. The great majority of detainees from Western Europe knew the camps only in this latter stage. Taken overall these consequences, so many and so serious, meant that unquestionably the camp system had undergone a revolution.

The camp network developed along two main lines of force. The central camps, powerful concentration complexes, were built along the lines of terror and its extensions. Economic necessities played no part in their foundation. They were the outcome of the increase of organised terror in Germany and of its extension, through the *Anschluss* and the war, to Central, Eastern, and Western Europe. The fixed *Kommandos*, set up as satellites to the large concentration complexes, were only for economic necessities, and their geographical distribution was dictated by the industrial infrastructure.

In 1936 the S.S. Death's Head units were restricted to fixed installations. This gave rise to the integrated complex: S.S. barracks–S.S. living quarters–concentration camp.

The three main S.S. camps were attached to the first three very powerful concentration complexes: Dachau near Munich, enlarged; Buchenwald near Weimar, founded in 1937; and Sachsenhausen, near Berlin.

The consolidation of Nazi power brought the creation of Gross Rosen in the Lausitz region; Flossenburg near Weiden in Bavaria; Neuengamme near Hamburg; and Ravensbrück in Mecklenburg. The *Anschluss* brought Mauthausen near Linz.

The war brought the development of the concentration camp network in Eastern Europe (Auschwitz, Treblinka, Sobibor, Maidanek, Belzek, Stutthof near Danzig), Natzweiler in the Vosges, Bergen-Belsen near Hannover, and Neubremm near Saarbrücken.

The crisis year of 1942 resulted in a network of satellite camps all over Ger-

△ *Mass burial for the bodies of those who died just before Auschwitz was liberated.*
◁ *The scene in Dachau when it was liberated by men of the U.S. 42nd (Rainbow) Division of the 7th Army early in May 1945. This camp, which served Bavaria, was one of the earliest to be set up, and here about 70,000 people had met their end. When the Americans entered the camp, they found many thousands of bodies lying there unburied.*

△ All that remained of the bodies of several hundred victims killed and cremated in Buchenwald.

taken of the "final solution". The true figure would appear to be between nine and ten million, probably nearer the latter.

Buchenwald was a typical large concentration camp complex. In April 1945 it had 47,500 detainees from 30 different countries and by that time several evacuations had taken place.

The camp at Lublin was the first to be freed by the Allies. Orders for the extermination of all camp inmates were sent out from Berlin, but there was such incoherence and confusion that they could not be complied with in the majority of cases. On January 18 Auschwitz was emptied. There was a slow exodus westwards to Buchenwald, Oranienburg, Mauthausen, Ravensbrück, Dachau, and Bergen-Belsen in open waggons and a temperature of minus 30 degrees Centigrade. The breakdown of relations with the outside and the influx of a fresh, harassed, and demented population completely disorganised the administration of the concentration camp complexes. There was total confusion as convoys of detainees, civilians, and troops crossed each other all over Germany. Famine spread and exanthematous typhus appeared. The S.S. went on killing. They killed on the roads all those who, in haggard columns, showed any signs of weakness. They killed indiscriminately. Even in its death-throes the world of the concentration camp accomplished its basic mission. The Nazi concentration camp system was broken when it was at its height. It did not collapse under the weight of the crumbling régime. It was broken from without by force of arms. The S.S. went down with Auschwitz and Buchenwald.

In *L'Univers concentrationnaire* and *Les Jours de notre Mort* I have described in detail life inside the camps. Here I have merely traced the outline of their history. From the outside I have seen them as one sees a comet. Here they belong to history and they make this history. The important thing is their genesis and their action on society. The lesson speaks to our intelligence. To understand this genesis and the changes brought about by the growth of the concentration camp system is of tremendous importance.

The sum of unspeakable sufferings cannot be weighed. It has nothing to do with historical analysis. It is not a social factor. It is the very depth of the camps' meaning. On this threshold the reader must listen to the witnesses.

many. There were about 900 in 1945 attached to 15 large centres.

The numbers of those detained are difficult to estimate because of the lack of sufficient documents. Eugen Kogon gives eight million, of whom seven and a half million died; he also says that in 12 years only 200,000 were set free.

Olga Wormser states that from 1933 to 1939 there were no more than 100,000 and that the total eventually reached five to six million, including survivors from Auschwitz (in 1945 these numbered only 65,000). She does not give figures for the victims of the "final solution", i.e. deportees who were gassed. Compared with Wormser's, Kogon's figures would appear to be high, but low if account is

Land warfare

The weapons with which the chief combatants began World War II were in many cases linear descendants of basic types that had seen service at the end of World War I.

Tanks and aircraft had been used together for combined attacks in 1918. They were used again at the beginning of World War II by the Germans in the novel tactical doctrine which became known as "Blitzkrieg".

These tactics, employed between 1939 and 1942, concealed the fact that the Germans still relied on horse-drawn vehicles and the marching power of their infantry to consolidate the gains won by the combination of tanks, Stuka dive-bombers, and motorised grenadiers.

Fortunately for the Germans, their enemies were either paralysed by "stand and fight" orders, or restricted to static linear defences. Tactical air strikes on the major lines of communication and airfields by dive-bombers and medium bombers added to the confusion which had been caused by feint attacks on selected points in the enemy's lines.

Then suddenly the full weight of the armoured assault would fall on a comparatively small sector of the front—the *Schwerpunkt* (point of main effort) of the attack.

Once the tanks and motorised infantry had broken through, they plunged into the open country headed by their armoured cars and motorcycle reconnaissance units. With them flew the Luftwaffe, acting as flying artillery. In great enveloping movements these forces would trap their enemy in pockets.

It was by concentrating their armour into Panzer divisions that the Germans gained an advantage over their opponents. For in both France and Russia their tanks were outnumbered and in some cases outclassed. But both France and Russia used tanks as a support arm for their infantry and scattered them along the front in troop- and squadron-sized units.

In the West the Germans had the added advantage of the excellent metalled roads which led deep into the enemy's

▽ The radio operator of a Panzerjäger "Marder III" gives covering fire with a captured Russian PPSh M1941 submachine gun. His companion is changing the magazine on his 7.92-mm MG 34 machine gun. The crew are members of the Waffen-S.S., and are wearing the characteristic camouflaged uniforms and caps of that organisation.

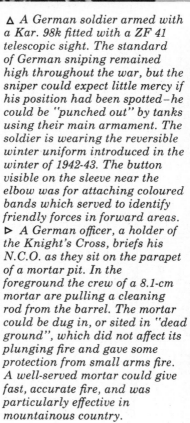

territory. In a few days' hard driving they could capture enough urban and industrial centres to make the continuation of the war impossible for their adversary.

In Russia they encountered appalling roads, vast spaces, and an extreme climate. The enormous size of the Soviet Union, its manpower, and its resources meant that it could take losses which would have crippled any Western nation. The Germans believed they were close to victory in 1941, and Hitler boasted "We have only to kick in the door and the whole rotten structure will come crashing down."

But in the winter, outside Moscow, the Blitzkrieg ran out of energy, and in sub-zero temperatures the Russians turned on their aggressors. In 1942 in the Ukraine the Germans again went on the offensive, but this time the Russians traded space for time, evading encirclement by their retreat to Stalingrad.

Here the German 6th Army was ground down in street by street, and even room by room, fighting. It was the antithesis of "lightning war".

In 1943 the Germans made one more major attack in the East, at Kursk in central Russia. Operation "Citadel" culminated in the biggest tank battle in history, and showed that deep field fortifications could halt the Blitzkrieg. Victory came with the Russian counter-attack which followed the German assault. But Kursk is unique, for the "Lucy" spy ring had supplied the Russians with almost all the German plans.

In anticipation the Russians laid out a system of defences in three lines. The first was up to three miles deep, the second was seven miles behind this, and the last line was 20 miles in the rear. The front was covered with a density of 2,400 anti-tank and 2,700 anti-personnel mines per mile, and the system supported by 6,000 anti-tank guns, 13,000 guns, and 1,000 rocket-launchers.

△ *A German soldier armed with a Kar. 98k fitted with a ZF 41 telescopic sight. The standard of German sniping remained high throughout the war, but the sniper could expect little mercy if his position had been spotted – he could be "punched out" by tanks using their main armament. The soldier is wearing the reversible winter uniform introduced in the winter of 1942-43. The button visible on the sleeve near the elbow was for attaching coloured bands which served to identify friendly forces in forward areas.*
▷ *A German officer, a holder of the Knight's Cross, briefs his N.C.O. as they sit on the parapet of a mortar pit. In the foreground the crew of a 8.1-cm mortar are pulling a cleaning rod from the barrel. The mortar could be dug in, or sited in "dead ground", which did not affect its plunging fire and gave some protection from small arms fire. A well-served mortar could give fast, accurate fire, and was particularly effective in mountainous country.*

◁ An MG sited in its curved weapon pit. The shape of the trench allowed the gunner to fire on an almost 360 degree front, while his crew could reload and feed in the ammunition belt. Also visible in the picture are two clips of rifle ammunition, and two St. Hgr. 24 stick grenades for close defence.

◁▽ Unusual transport for the Blitzkrieg: a rifle section rides on two railway maintenance cars in Yugoslavia. Behind the officer (checking his map) is the machine gunner, with his gas cape case on his chest.

▽ A paratrooper sprints forward with his MP 40 sub-machine gun. Known incorrectly to the Allies as the Schmeisser, the sub-machine gun was first issued to specialist troops, but was later carried by army N.C.O.s.

2440

◁ ◁ *The contradictions of the German Army in the Blitzkrieg period. In the foreground 8-ton half-track Sd.Kfz. 7 prime movers tow 15-cm guns, but in the background teams of horses and limbers can be seen with 10.5-cm le. F.H. 18 howitzers.*

◁ *An MG 34 on an anti-aircraft tripod mounting. It is fitted with a 50-round drum magazine, and an A.A. ring sight.*

◁▽ *A Junkers Ju 52 transport aircraft during the first winter in Russia. A section has piled its arms and waits to load stores.*

▽ *Happier days in Russia. German troops have debussed from their trucks after coming under fire during the advance in the summer of 1941.*

2442

About 40 miles behind this system, the front reserves, ready to go over to the counter-offensive, had dug their own entrenched defence line.

Before considering Germany on the defensive, it is worth examining the partisan war behind her front line. The mountains, swamps, and forests of Europe could conceal large numbers of men (and women), and could only be approached along a few restricted roads. From these natural havens the *maquis*, partisans, and other resistance groups could attack the Axis lines of communication, and even overwhelm small local garrisons.

In the ruthless war in the East it was difficult for civilians to remain neutral when each side executed or murdered its opponents on capturing new territory. As the war swung against the Axis, the partisan bands expanded to become units based on regular army lines.

The prospect of liberation helped the partisan cause, though some men joined through self-interest and self-preservation in the later years.

In the mountains of Yugo-

◁ ◁ *German gunners on an island on the North Sea coast traverse their gun. The position is draped with camouflage nets, a precaution which became increasingly necessary as the Allies gained air superiority.*

◁ *Under cover of smoke, German troops rise from their positions to go in to the attack. This picture was taken on a training exercise mounted before the troops went up the line to the Eastern Front. Before important operations, picked troops would practise for months on full scale models of their objectives.*

▽ *An American soldier examines a knocked out Sd.Kfz. 173 "Jagdpanther". It has been hit in the centre of its tracks and has then caught fire. The "Jagdpanther" was probably the finest S.P. tank destroyer to be produced by the Germans. It combined the powerful 8.8-cm anti-tank gun with a low silhouette and the successful Panther chassis.*

◁ ◁ U.S. troops with a battered and abandoned "Sturmtiger". This vehicle was developed after the German experience of fighting in Stalingrad. The army called for a 21-cm howitzer for close support against difficult targets. The Raketenwerfer 61 L/54, a 38-cm rocket projector, was finally proposed and about ten Tiger tanks were converted to take this unusual weapon.

▽ ◁ A mixed group of Wehrmacht and Waffen-S.S. personnel riding in an N.S.U. Kettenkrad half-track motorcycle. Developed for airborne forces, it could tow light field guns or weapons containers.

◁ An officer stands on the hull and hands down the ammunition as the crew reload a German self-propelled gun. They are wearing the field grey uniform with double-breasted jacket peculiar to tank destroyer and S.P. assault gun crews.

▽ A 7.5-cm Sturmgeschütz 40 grinds past a Waffen-S.S. trooper. The assault gun crew have fixed a large wooden box to the rear deck of their vehicle to stow their kit.

slavia and the Massif Central of France, German and Axis forces used artillery, tanks, and aircraft in vast cordon and search operations to root out resistance.

In defence, the Germans drew on the expertise that had built the pre-war *Autobahns*. The Todt Organisation erected the Atlantic Wall, the *Westwall* or Siegfried Line, and the Gustav and Gothic Lines. To these the Wehrmacht added field fortifications and obstacles.

Parts of these systems remain intact today, mute tribute to the German engineers and their conscripted labourers.

The *Westwall* was the most developed line. Massive concrete bunkers were sited in depth along the border with France, so that each could give supporting fire when they came under attack. The bunkers were gas-proof, and equipped with quarters for their garrisons, their own power supply, and weapons which included machine guns, mortars, and field and anti-tank guns. They were dug into hillsides and railway embankments, disguised as farm buildings and houses, and had large trees transplanted and positioned on or around them. In addition, belts of mines, barbed wire, and dragon's teeth anti-

tank obstacles scarred the German fields along the French border.

In 1939 the *Westwall* had a sufficiently awesome reputation to discourage the French from attacking. But defences are only as good as the troops manning them, and when the Germans attacked the outworks of the Maginot Line at Sedan in 1940, they hit an area held by low grade reservists.

The paratroops who held the Gustav Line at Monte Cassino blocked the Allied advance in 1943 and 1944 longer than the elderly reservists and sailors who manned the neglected em-

placements on the *Westwall* in 1944 and 1945.

Fixed defences are like river lines–once they are breached they cease to be of any value, for the whole system can be rolled up from behind. Given the time, the men, the means, and most of all the will, any system can be breached if its garrison remains passively defensive.

General George Patton visited the *Westwall* after its capture and was surprised by the limited fire-power of some of the emplacements. He learned that the Americans had been able to knock them out by smothering the embrasures with small arms fire and placing a dynamite charge against the back door, or by using self-propelled 155-mm guns at short range. "At three hundred yards the 155 shell will remove a pillbox for every round fired," he explained.

For the British and their allies the early years of the war were grim times, distinguished only by the victories over the Italians in Abyssinia and North Africa, and a series of fighting retreats from Europe. Despite this, they retained cohesion in the face of attacks by the most professional army the world had known. Indeed on Crete they came close to defeating the German paratroop attack, made by a force that Churchill described as "the flame of the Hitler Youth Movement... an ardent embodiment of the Teutonic spirit of revenge for the defeat of 1918".

In retreat the British formed all-arm *ad hoc* units which took

◁ A 2-cm Flakvierling 38 mounted on a half track 8-ton Sd.Kfz. 7. With one man on watch the rest of the crew relaxes.
▽ ◁ A 10.5-cm anti-aircraft gun on a coastal mounting.

▷ An Sd.Kfz. 251 half-track, mounting a PaK 36/37 3.7-cm anti-tank gun. Panzergrenadier platoon commanders were issued with this vehicle to give them increased battlefield firepower.
▽ ▷ A 3.7-cm anti-aircraft gun with 14 kill rings on the barrel. Throughout the war the Germans were capable of putting up a heavy anti-aircraft barrage at very short notice.

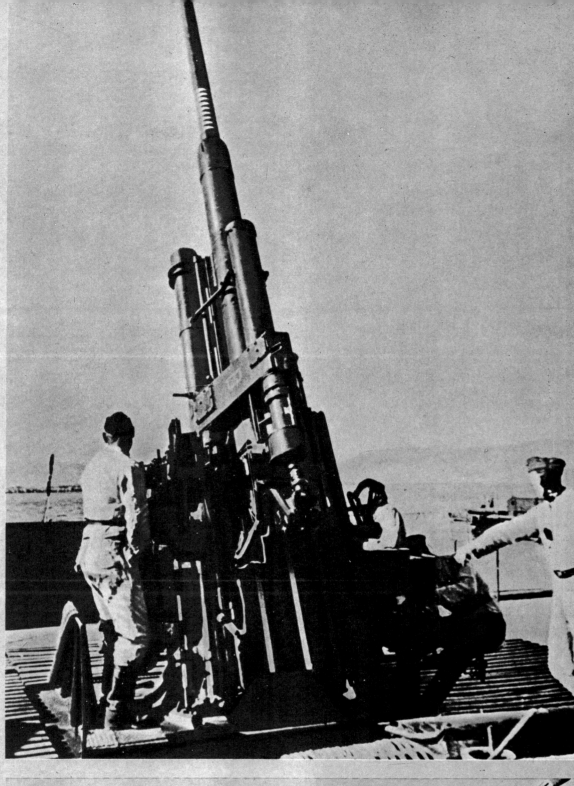

▷ *A Volkswagen Kdf. 82*
Kübelwagen *outside Bizerta*
in January 1943. The
Kübelwagen *was the German*
equivalent of the Jeep, but had
the added advantage of an
air-cooled engine.

▽ *A "brewed up" Panther*
Ausf. A. It has been strung with
chicken wire for attaching
camouflage garnish.
▷ *A British Army training*
poster. Lecture rooms and
barracks displayed this type of
poster which served both to
exhort and instruct. But
ultimately it was the front line
which confirmed the value of
battle craft.

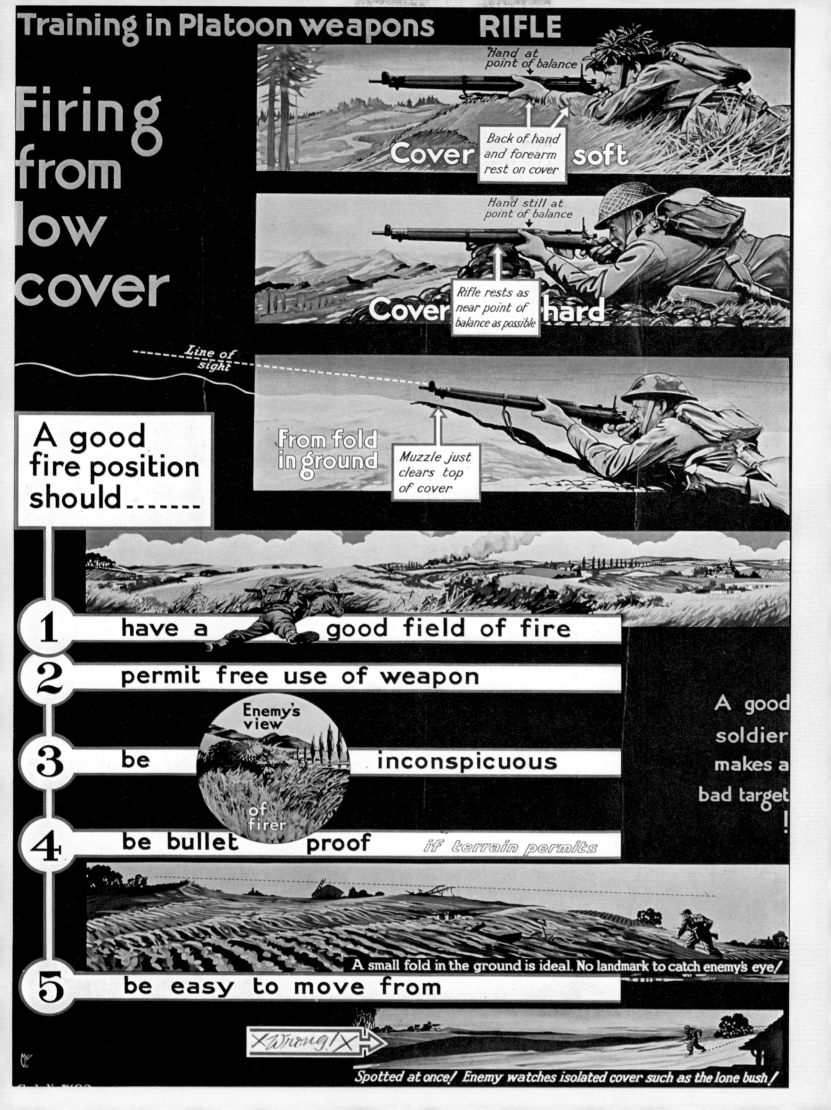

Firing from low cover

Hand at point of balance

Back of hand and forearm rest on cover

Cover soft

Hand still at point of balance

Rifle rests as near point of balance as possible

Cover hard

Line of sight

From fold in ground

Muzzle just clears top of cover

A good fire position should ....

1 have a good field of fire

2 permit free use of weapon

Enemy's view

3 be inconspicuous

of firer

4 be bullet proof *if terrain permits*

A good soldier makes a bad target!

A small fold in the ground is ideal. No landmark to catch enemy's eye!

5 be easy to move from

XWrong!X ➔

Spotted at once! Enemy watches isolated cover such as the lone bush!

▷ A British gun crew in Egypt in June 1940. After the gas attacks of World War I, all the combatants were trained and equipped for gas warfare.

▷ ▷ "Wasp" flame-throwers demonstrate their equipment. The Wasp was one of the many versions of the basic tracked Universal Carrier.

▽ British Grant tanks and armoured cars in North Africa, during a briefing.

▽ ▽ A 6-pounder anti-tank gun en portée. Carried like this, the gun had greater mobility, and could be brought up quickly to provide an anti-tank screen.

▷ ▽ A Vickers machine gun crew during a drill in 1940. The sergeant is about to give the signal to fire, which will be passed on to the gunner by his Number Two with a tap on the shoulder.

▷ ▷ ▽ British Covenanter Cruiser Tanks Mk. V during training in southern England. Although it did not see much action, this type served extensively as a training vehicle.

the name of their commanding officer. Later the Germans adopted the same system, calling the units *Kampfgruppen*. Finally they made these formations a regular feature of their operations, and *Kampfgruppe* "Peiper", part of the 1st S.S. Panzer Division, featured prominently in the Ardennes offensive.

All the combatant nations taught small unit tactics as drills. This meant that just as a man could strip and clean his weapon almost without looking, so in an emergency a corporal would instinctively use all the available fire-power in his section.

All drills and plans, however, have to be adapted to circumstances, and from the Corporal to the General there was always a feeling that with a few more resources the job would be easier.

For lack of hand grenades the "bombers" in a house clearing team would have to rake a room with sub-machine gun fire. In North Africa each side tried to conceal its tank strength, or lack of it, by using soft skinned vehicles to stir up dust clouds to resemble tanks on the move.

North Africa was a proving ground for British generalship and Allied co-operation. The Army

had its revenge at Alamein, while the Americans armed, supported, and later rivalled their battle-wise Allies.

After the Allied victory in Africa, the war in Europe was punctuated by a series of major amphibious operations, which reached a climax in the D-Day landings in Normandy.

Experience at Dieppe, in Sicily and in Italy prompted the British to develop a series of close support weapons and specialised armour. Batteries of rockets fired from special landing craft would saturate a beach area 750 yards by 160 with 5-inch projectiles.

With the first wave of landing craft an array of armoured "Funnies" rumbled into action against the obstacles and enemy emplacements. They carried bridges, flame-throwers, demolition charges, rolls of hessian matting to provide a path over the sand, and flails to explode the mine-fields. Some conventional tanks swam ashore using flotation skirts and a special drive off the engine.

After the beach had been secured, flotillas of D.U.K.W. amphibious trucks brought men and stores to inland parks.

A huge range of landing craft

▷ On the 2nd Baltic Front, January 1945: Soviet "Katyusha" rockets are moved up. Lacking the accuracy of conventional artillery, they were, however, an efficient psychological weapon, with a high blast effect.

▽ A German soldier stacks captured Russian 14.5-mm anti-tank rifles. Single shot weapons, they could penetrate 1.2 inches of armour at 500 yards.

▷ ▽ The Russian armoured train "Ilya Muromets" in the fighting near Warsaw in 1944. The train is armed with T-34 turrets. In the foreground the railway sleepers have been torn up by a German track demolition device.

and prefabricated equipment enabled the Allies to establish port facilities and build airstrips. Later, at the assault river crossings of the Rhine, and operations in Walcheren and northern Italy, tracked landing vehicles which had been developed for the island hopping campaigns in the Pacific were used.

Fighter, medium, and even heavy bombers provided tactical support with awesome effects, and in the early days of the landings warships put broadsides into targets as small as a football pitch.

For all these resources and originality, the western Allies never produced tanks which combined an efficient gun with adequate armour. Though their tanks were faster and more mobile than later German types, they were easy to knock out, and the Sherman was given the grisly nicknames of "Ronson" and "Tommy Cooker" by the German gunners because of its tendency to catch fire when hit.

With the complete control of the air by the Allies, the Germans were forced to operate by night. Their anti-tank guns were moved up, sited, and camouflaged in the darkness, but in the "battle of the hedgerows" in Normandy they knocked out the Allied tanks which had moved up freely during the day.

Yet for every 8.8-cm gun lurking in the *bocage,* there were batteries of British and American guns. In the 25-pounder, the British and Allies had a weapon which could serve in either an anti-tank or a conventional rôle. The Americans co-ordinated their fire through a Fire Direction Centre, which enabled them to fire Time on Targets barrage, in which the shells of 100 or more guns would land on the same target at the same time.

In the latter half of the war the Germans still retained a high standard of artillery marksmanship by use of sound and flash location troops and by intercepting radio traffic.

Impressive as an artillery barrage might seem to those who fired or received it, the mortar and mine emerged from the war in the West as among the most efficient killers.

Yet however efficient the weapons, they still needed men to crew or operate them. The generation of officers who held high command in World War II had served in the previous war as junior officers, and from that experience had learned the importance of leadership and morale.

Men were trained to work as a team, from the section with its Bren gun or L.M.G. to the corps or army group with all its supporting arms. In the end, all types of attack are based on the "fire and movement" principle in which the enemy is pinned down by fire, while the assault group moves into a position from which it can rush forward when the fire lifts and overcome the enemy. In any variant of this manoeuvre each half of the team, whatever its size, has to understand its rôle and carry it out effectively.

For the Allies the war was a crusade to liberate occupied Europe. For the Germans the war with Russia was another crusade, to save Europe from the "Slavic sub-humans". The intense ideological emotions generated by the conflict help,

▷ *German officers examine an M3A5 tank knocked out by a Pzkw VI Tiger in North Africa.*
▽ *A Sherman tank fitted with rollers to detonate anti-tank mines. If covered by fire, a minefield could not be lifted by hand, and had to be cleared by special armoured vehicles.*

▲▷ *Men of the 83rd Division of the U.S. 9th Army prepare to fire captured German 28-cm rockets on a position in a factory on the east bank of the Rhine. The rockets had a range of 2,300 yards and carried a warhead of 110 lbs of T.N.T. or Amatol.*
▽▷ *A U.S. 81-mm mortar in action in France. The officer is checking the ranges over the field telephone.*
▽▷▷ *A park of captured German 7.5-cm anti-tank guns in France.*

▷ *An M4 Sherman fitted with a flame-thrower in place of the bow machine gun.*
▷ ▷ *A soldier of the U.S. Chemical Warfare Service with his M1 flame gun. Allied flame-throwers, unlike German weapons, could project unignited fuel through a bunker embrasure, and then follow it with a burst of flame.*

▽ *A height-finder crew during training in the United States.*
▷ ▽ *A demonstration of an M1 flame gun against a bunker. If the occupants were not caught in the flames, they were overcome when the oxygen inside the emplacement was exhausted.*

in part, to explain the courage, fanaticism, and brutality of the fighting.

In the Winter War with Finland in 1939, neither the Russian soldier nor his equipment had proved superior to the Finns. It was only by massed attacks that they had broken through the Mannerheim Line, and at heavy human and *matériel* loss forced an armistice on the Finns. Encouraged by this demonstration of military ineptitude, the Germans believed that their superior tactics and equipment would take them to Moscow before winter.

Defending his own homeland, the Russian soldier showed a toughness and stubborn determination which came as a considerable shock. Machine gunners would hide up, and long after the tanks had passed, open fire on the soft-skinned supply

vehicles following in the rear.

When the Panzers had encircled pockets of Russian soldiers some would try to fight their way out, or go to ground as partisans.

In the early months of the war, it was not the soldiers but their leaders who were to blame for the huge Russian losses. Counter-attacks were badly prepared, and the men were sent on one-way charges in closely packed lines, which provided ideal, and ultimately sickening, target practice for the Germans. Even the T-34, whose appearance produced a "tank terror" among the Germans, was squandered in penny-packet tactics.

By the time the German armour had reached the approaches to Moscow, its support and supply echelons were bogged down miles to the rear in the mud and slush of the Russian autumn. The only advances could be made by in-

△ Caught at the wrong end of a rifle. Two U.S. medical corpsmen treat a wounded infantryman during the fighting in Sicily.

▷ An American landing craft loaded with wounded after the D-Day landings.

▷▷ During training at Edgewood Arsenal, Maryland, troops use M2-2 manpack flame-throwers in a simulated attack. They are covered by two men with Browning Automatic Rifles. Allied flame-throwers were designed to produce a bushy flame which was found to have greater psychological effect.

fantry on foot. When the winter came, it was against these exhausted and underclad men that the Russians launched their fresh Siberian troops. Not only were they fresh troops, they were equipped with weapons and vehicles adapted to conditions of severe cold, and dressed in warm quilted uniforms. The threat to Moscow was averted, but the Red Army lacked the logistic facilities to permit them to follow up their breakthroughs with their own Blitzkrieg tactics.

In the year following, 1942, the Russians were again defending a city, but this time it was street fighting. At Stalingrad the lines were so close that the Luftwaffe was unable to provide support for fear of hitting their own men. The Russians fought with a determination that at first enraged and later terrified their opponents. Small "storm groups" would make their way through the sewers and gullies which led up from the river, and appear behind the German lines. Other groups would hold out in industrial plants and warehouses and fight until their ammunition was exhausted. In addition to these groups, snipers added to the hazards of the Germans.

When the Russians came to launch their counter-attack at Stalingrad, they preceded it with a massive artillery bombardment. What they lost in accuracy they made up for in density. The weaker units like the Italians and Rumanians were subject to fire

The "Fire and Movement" team in action; the rifle man moves in to occupy the ground.
▷ U.S. infantrymen enter the village of Marigny in France. They are festooned with bandoliers of ammunition, and the man in the foreground has a rifle grenade fitted to his M1 Garand semi-automatic rifle.
▷▷ In the bocage fighting, American soldiers dash across an exposed road under rifle fire. In the background is a knocked out Skoda 175 wheeled tractor, and in the foreground a Panther tank.

▽ Street fighting in the French village of Saintenay. American soldiers approach cautiously after throwing a smoke grenade to conceal themselves from any enemy remaining in the houses.

△ *The culmination of "Fire and Movement" on an international scale. A shattered 8.8-cm gun in the square in front of the Reichstag in Berlin, on May 7, 1945. The city had been hit by Bomber Command and the U.S. Army Air Force during the war, and blasted street by street by the Red Army in its battle for the capital of the Reich.*

from 13,500 guns and mortars of all calibres, plus demoralising salvoes of 130-mm Katyusha rockets with their 48-lb high explosive warheads.

The same spirit which had characterised the Red Army in defence now carried it forward in attack. Tank riding infantrymen, armed with sub-machine guns, overwhelmed what remained of the Axis infantry. Unlike the lavishly equipped Western armies, the Russians practised a stricter economy with their equipment and supplies than they did with the lives of their men. Attacks were sometimes sent in so that the Germans would open fire and so reveal their hidden gun emplacements which would then come under counter-battery fire.

In the last days in Berlin this same ruthlessness showed in the Russian determination to take the capital. 203-mm howitzers were brought up to blast buildings at point blank range. Guns were moved up with each advance, positioned in any available open space and Berlin was burned and blasted with white phosphorus and high explosive.

In 1945 the tactical lessons of nearly seven years of fighting were still true. The Blitzkrieg concept of deep penetration by massed armour and motorised infantry had returned to plague its original practitioners. The Germans were faced in the West by Allied armies which were completely mechanised and supported by a formidable air force. In the East were tanks rivalled only by the latest German types, in numbers undreamt of by the Panzer generals even in the early days of the war.

But from what remained of Germany's airfields and *Autobahns* the world's first operational jet fighters and bombers made a brief and spectacular appearance over the front. 1,115 V-2 liquid-fuelled rockets had fallen on Britain, and four months after V.E. Day the first atomic bomb fell on Hiroshima. The victor of the next war would be the survivor who recovered first.

Air warfare

Although aircraft had been used in previous wars, notably World War I, the Spanish Civil War, the Japanese invasion of China, and the Italian campaign against Abyssinia, it was only in World War II that air power began to show its true potentialities.

This is not to say that the rôle aircraft might play had not been foreseen by the theorists of air power. Men such as the British Trenchard and Sykes, the Italian Douhet, the American Mitchell, and the Russian/American Sever-

sky had all devoted much of their lives to anticipating the rôle of the bomber fleets they imagined would be the ultimate "strategic" weapon in the next war. But they were wrong. Estimates of hundreds of thousands dead in a few days of concentrated bombardment were proved erroneous in the London "Blitz" and in the late-war Allied bombardment of German cities: the power of conventional high explosive bombs had been overestimated very considerably, and the will to resist on

△ A Supermarine Spitfire VC of No. 303 (Polish) Squadron, R.A.F. Fighter Command. Noteworthy are the Polish chequer on the nose, the 18-inch wide "sky" band round the rear fuselage (indicating that the aircraft was a day fighter), the spinner in the same colour, and the 6-inch wide yellow stripe along the wings' leading edges, introduced in September 1941. The Spitfire proved a superlative and adaptable weapon right through the war and was flown with very considerable success by the aggressive Poles.

the part of the civilian population underestimated even more. The men left at home had many of them served in the trenches in World War I, and therefore knew how to survive intensive bombardment. This is not to say that bombing was not successful in the strategic rôle–an assessment of the Allies' destruction of the German transport, synthetic rubber, and petroleum industries will provide ample proof of how effective this was in finally humbling the Third Reich. The Allies' mistake lay in realising too late that these were the true strategic targets against which they should be directing their bomber efforts. It was not until the advent of nuclear weapons, and the atom bombings of Hiroshima and Nagasaki, that air power became a true strategic or grand strategic weapon.

Be that as it may, aircraft played an increasingly important part in the war in the European Theatre of Operations (E.T.O.). When the war started, Germany possessed a decided superiority in the air. This does not imply that all her aircraft were superior to those in Allied service, but that her aircraft were entirely adequate for the tasks intended for them, and that the tactics to be used had been thought out and practised carefully, in the Spanish Civil War and in peace-time Germany. First line strength was some 4,840 (including 1,750 medium bombers and 1,200 fighters) with a reserve of similar numbers and an aircraft industry capable of turning out 1,100 aircraft per month.

Great Britain had a similar number of aircraft, but most of these were obsolete fighters and obsolescent bombers, with only about 1,000 modern fighters avail-

able. But this last figure was the important one, as the country was geared to the defensive. Here the fighters, aided by radar, could defend the nation in the difficult days before an adequate strike force could be built up. More importantly, better designs were on the drawing boards and would be in action before Germany realised the error of her ways in planning only for a short war.

France's position in the air was very poor. In numbers her air force was weak, with only some 1,400 combat aircraft. For during the 1930's France had let the equipment of her air force gradually decline in standard, and it was only when it was too late that she realised that an up-to-date air force was necessary in a modern war. By then it was too late, and although some excellent designs were produced

Although its design was older than the Spitfire's, the Hawker Hurricane also proved a worthy fighter, shooting down more aircraft in the Battle of Britain than all other British fighters combined.

◁ *The Royal Navy's version – Sea Hurricane IA.*

▽ ◁ *The Hurricane IID, armed with two 40-mm cannon. This saw action for the first time in North Africa on June 6, 1942, and soon became the scourge of Axis armour.*

▽ *Probably the best heavy bomber of the war – Britain's Avro Lancaster. This is a Mark I of No. 50 Squadron, R.A.F. Bomber Command. The major failing of the type was lack of adequate defensive armament: few Lancasters were fitted with ventral guns, and the rest were all .303-inch ones.*

The British Bristol Beaufighter Torpedo Fighter X

Engines: two Bristol Hercules XVII radials,
1,770-hp each.
Armament: four 20-mm Hispano cannon
with 283 rounds per gun and one .303-inch
Vickers K gun, plus one 1,650- or 2,127-lb
torpedo and two 250-lb bombs or eight
60-lb rockets.
Speed: 303 mph at 1,300 feet.
Ceiling: 15,000 feet.
Range: 1,470 miles.
Weight empty/loaded: 15,600/25,200 lbs.
Span: 57 feet 10 inches.
Length: 41 feet 8 inches.
Height: 15 feet 10 inches.
Crew: 2.

▷ *Spitfires of the Allied air armada en route to Normandy in 1944. Already in service at the beginning of the war, the Spitfire had been developed from the Mark I eight .303-inch machine gun, 365 mph interceptor fighter into the Mark XIVE two 20-mm cannon- and two .5-inch machine gun- (plus 1,000-lb bomb-load) armed 448 mph fighter-bomber. During this time the loaded weight of the aircraft had increased from 5,784 to 8,500 pounds and the horsepower available from the Merlin III (1,030) had increased to that of the Griffon 65 (2,050). Yet the handling characteristics of the machine altered relatively little, with control in roll still very heavy at high speed.*

▽ *Possibly a propaganda photograph faked up by the Germans: an early mark of Spitfire flashes past the nose of a Heinkel 111 medium bomber.*

▷ *Part of the Allied day and night bomber offensive: Boeing B-17F's of the U.S. 8th Air Force approach the Dornier factory at Meulan in France above cloud cover. Combat experience with the F model led to the G, which had a twin .5-inch chin turret to counter the German fighters' favourite ploy, the head-on attack.*

▷ ▷ *The other mainstay of the American heavy day bomber offensive: Consolidated B-24's cross the North Sea on their way to Germany. The aircraft belong to the 458th Bombardment Group of the 2nd Air Division's 96th Combat Wing.*

▽ *Result of combat experience: the chin turret-armed B-17G.*

▽ ▷ *Britain's first four-engined heavy bomber, the ungainly Short Stirling, posed beside a Bf 109 on a German airfield.*

▽ ▽ ▷ *The excellent Wellington.*

in 1939 and 1940, few examples had attained operational status. Training was good, however, and despite the drawback of their equipment, French pilots gave a good account of themselves in the air.

Finally, of the major powers involved in the war's early stages, there was Italy's air force. Here, as with the Germans, Italian pilots had the decided advantage of combat experience in the Spanish Civil War, but their high command had drawn virtually all the wrong conclusions from the campaign. Biplane fighters were still considered adequate, and medium bombers sufficient for Italy's aims. With some 5,000 aircraft (including reserves), however, the Italian Air Force was numerically strong. The total included some 1,000 each of bombers and fighters, and 750 reconnaissance and transport machines.

At this time, the distinction between the various types of aircraft was fairly rigid: the fighter was purely a defensive machine, intended to oppose the enemy's bombers; the light bomber was intended to support ground operations, with reconnaissance aircraft providing the information on which they could act; medium bombers operated well behind the enemy's lines; and maritime aircraft undertook reconnaissance and attack tasks

at sea.

The Germans, as is now well known, were the best exponents of this almost purely tactical concept of air war. Their experience in the Spanish Civil War had confirmed their earlier theories that the use of aircraft as flying artillery for their rapidly-advancing ground forces was the best way to ensure success. Combined with this was the very important point that to operate at low level in direct support of the army, it was necessary to provide totally effective fighter cover. Here the Germans excelled—again, combat over Spain had led them to abandon the rigid formations that had characterised World War I operations, in favour of a loose basic formation of four aircraft (Schwarm), which divided into two pairs (Rotten) of lead pilot and wingman. This ensured the right combination of flexibility and combat safety, with the wingman protecting his leader's rear.

This then was the origin of the aerial side of the "Blitzkrieg", which swept all before it during the Polish campaign in 1939, the sea- and air-borne invasions of Denmark and Norway in 1940, and the attack on the Low Countries and France, again in 1940. Surprise and accuracy once again proved their paramount importance.

The Germans came unstuck in

△ ◁ *Classic ground-attack fighter, the Hawker Typhoon. Armed with four 20-mm cannon and eight 60-lb rockets, this was more than a match for any German tank of World War II.*
▽ ◁ *The magnificent Bristol Beaufighter strike-fighter. Heavy but immensely strong, the Beaufighter could carry a powerful offensive load – used in the anti-shipping rôle, its eight rockets were the equivalent of a broadside from a 6-inch cruiser.*
△ *The cockpit of "General Ike", a B-17G of the 401st Bombardment Group, 1st Combat Wing, 1st Air Division, christened by Eisenhower in April 1944.*
◁ *Fin and rudder of a Short Sunderland III anti-submarine patrol aircraft.*
▽ *Hawker Typhoon.*

the Battle of Britain, however. No longer was the Luftwaffe acting as a tactical adjunct of the army at short and easily-controlled ranges, but rather attempting to fulfil a purely strategic rôle. Admittedly, the Battle had started with what might be considered "grand tactical" operations against the Royal Air Force, in an effort to clear the way for the army. But this soon gave way to the strategic efforts of the "Blitz". The Luftwaffe's task was an impossible one: the bombers had the range to attack most of the worthwhile targets in Great Britain, but being designed for a different type of mission did not have the bomb-load to cause mortal damage. But the bombers were also incapable of defending themselves by day, and thus required fighter escort. Germany's fighters, however, had been designed for short range missions. Even operating from forward bases on the Channel coast, the Bf 109's and 110's could loiter over southern England for only 30 minutes, and over London for only ten. The offensive was thus doomed to failure. The night Blitz posed fewer problems, but again the

tonnage dropped was too small to break the Londoners' will, and night navigation became very difficult after the British had devised means of disrupting the German radio navigation systems.

British results in the early stages of the Battle of Britain were not particularly good, as a result of the pilots' lack of combat experience and an over-adherence to rigid formation attacks. As the battle continued, however, the lessons of experience were assimilated, and the looser German tactical formations adopted. Thus when the British went over to the offensive, launching fighter sweeps over occupied France in 1941, the success ratio was quite good. The range of fighter aircraft was still too low for genuine offensive missions, and strenuous efforts were made by both the British and the Germans to develop droppable fuel tanks to extend fighter ranges. As R.A.F. Fighter Command began to take the war to Germany, Bomber Command was also stepping up its efforts—with notable lack of success. For as with the Germans' Blitz bombing, the British were forced to

◁ ◁ The best Allied fighter of the war: the magnificent North American P-51D long-range fighter and fighter bomber. Originally designed to a British requirement and fitted with an Allison inline engine, the Mustang proved to be a good low level machine. But fitted with a Merlin engine its performance was spectacular. The D model had the adequate top of 437 mph, but the excellent range of 2,080 miles (which enabled it to escort bombers to Berlin and back), plus six .5-inch machine guns and in the ground attack rôle up to 2,000-lbs of bombs or ten 5-inch rockets.

◁ ◁ The largest and heaviest single-seat and engined fighter of World War II: the massive Republic P-47 Thunderbolt. This is a D model, the first to have a bubble canopy.

▽ The North American B-25 Mitchell medium bomber.

The British de Havilland Mosquito Fighter-Bomber VI

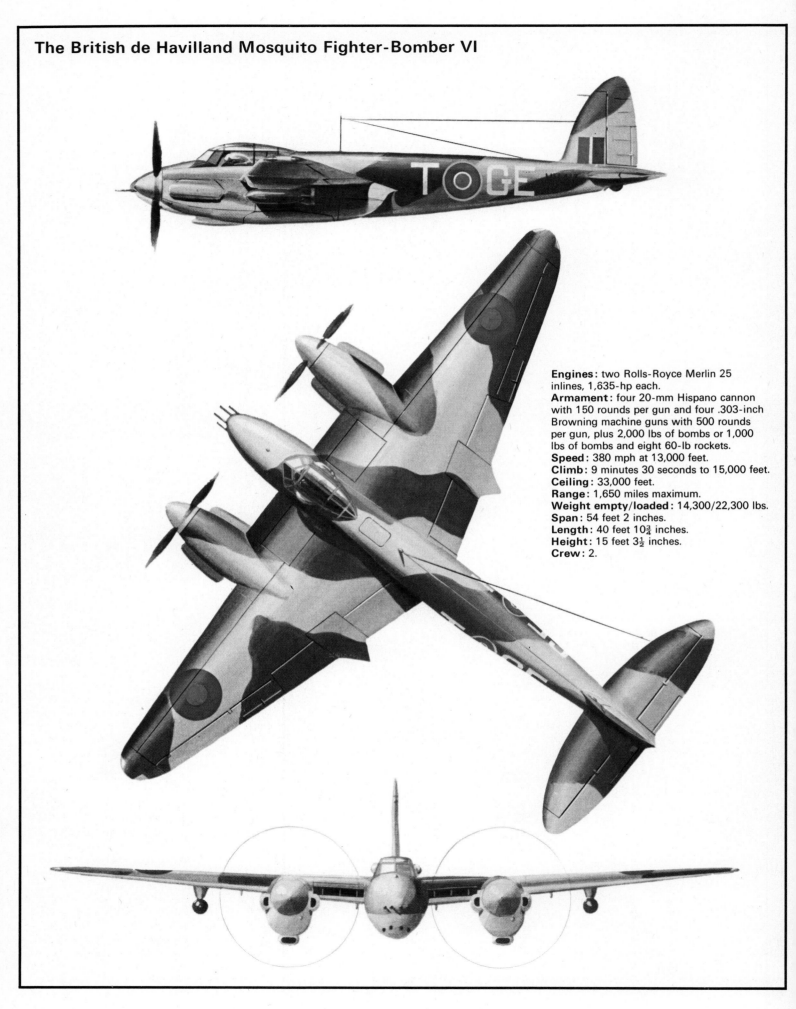

Engines: two Rolls-Royce Merlin 25 inlines, 1,635-hp each.
Armament: four 20-mm Hispano cannon with 150 rounds per gun and four .303-inch Browning machine guns with 500 rounds per gun, plus 2,000 lbs of bombs or 1,000 lbs of bombs and eight 60-lb rockets.
Speed: 380 mph at 13,000 feet.
Climb: 9 minutes 30 seconds to 15,000 feet.
Ceiling: 33,000 feet.
Range: 1,650 miles maximum.
Weight empty/loaded: 14,300/22,300 lbs.
Span: 54 feet 2 inches.
Length: 40 feet $10\frac{3}{4}$ inches.
Height: 15 feet $3\frac{1}{2}$ inches.
Crew: 2.

fly by night to avoid heavy losses, and navigation was so poor that very few bombers ever arrived over their intended targets. The only real benefits were the experience gained at this earlier stage in the game, and an increase in civilian morale.

In June 1941, the Germans made their biggest mistake since starting the war and attacked Soviet Russia. The latter had more than 8,000 combat aircraft at the time, and a large proportion of these were destroyed in the first few weeks of war. But they were mostly obsolete or obsolescent, and in a way the Germans did the Russians a favour. Russia was now able to devote her considerable energies to re-equipping her air force with more modern types. These were, until the closing stages of the war, qualitatively worse than contemporary German and other Allied types, but nonetheless entirely adequate for the tasks intended.

The Russians, with no ambitions in the field of strategic bombing, produced virtually nothing but tactical machines such as the superlative Ilyushin Il-2m3 and Petlyakov Pe-2, plus vast numbers of sturdy, well-armed, low-altitude fighters, which co-operated with the army in driving the Germans back out of Russia right the way back to Berlin. Russian aircrew standards never

matched the best that the Germans could produce, but contrary to the common impression, by the end of the war Soviet pilots were of a high and capable general standard. German air strength was gradually and inevitably ground away over the Eastern Front.

Back in the West, the strategic initiative was swinging gradually but decisively towards Great Britain and the United States, now that the latter had been brought into the war by the Japanese blow at Pearl Harbor. The aerial forces deployed by the U.S. were considerable, and of a high standard of *matériel* and training. Previously the U.S. had supplied large numbers of aircraft to the Allies under Lend-Lease, and in return had been informed about combat conditions prevailing over Europe. Thus when American forces began to operate over the continent, their success was fair, with the exception of disastrous raids such as the Regensburg and Schweinfurt attacks. The most immediate contribution made by the Americans, however, was in helping to close the notorious "Atlantic Gap" from the Western side.

The British were also improving at the same time. 1942 saw the arrival of the first true heavy bombers into service, and the raid on Cologne, the first "1,000-

bomber raid" on the night of May 30–31, 1942, heralded the steady growth of the R.A.F.'s strategic bomber offensive against Germany. But although heavy damage was caused, British losses became heavier as the Germans developed more efficient radar and night fighter defences. Matters only improved later in the war with the introduction on the British side of more sophisticated air-borne radar and long-range night intruders (such as versions of the de Havilland Mosquito) to take on the German night fighters. Only then did losses to the Lancaster, Halifax, and Wellington fleets decline.

The R.A.F.'s night efforts against the more vulnerable but less important "area" targets were complemented by the day attacks launched by the U.S.A.

△ △ *Hawker Tempest II fighter-bomber. The Tempest was conceived as a successor to the Typhoon, with a more powerful engine and improved aerodynamics and structural integrity. Two main versions of the Tempest appeared: first the Mark V, fitted with a 2,200-hp Napier Sabre inline, and then the Mark II, with a 2,500-hp Bristol Centaurus radial. The Mark II was a very useful machine, with a top speed of 440 mph and an offensive load of 2,000 lbs in addition to its four 20-mm cannon, but was just too late to see service.*
△ *The American Lockheed Lightning long-range fighter, easily distinguishable by its twin booms, central nacelle for the pilot, and boom-mounted empennage.*

2478

△ ◁ *Messerschmitt Bf 110 heavy fighters of 1 Staffel, I Gruppe, Schnelles Kampfgeschwader 210 (1st Squadron, 1st Wing, 210th Fast Bomber Group). Designed as a heavy bomber destroyer, the Bf 110 was pressed into service at the beginning of the war as a long range fighter, as which it proved very vulnerable to British single-engined fighters. But as the Allied bomber fleets started to pound Germany, the 110 began to be used in its true rôle by day and night and showed itself to be more than adequate for its tasks.*

◁ ◁ *The wreckage of a shot-down Junkers Ju 88. This, one of the most versatile aircraft of the war, was used as a medium bomber, maritime reconnaissance, torpedo-bomber, minelayer, fighter, ground attack, and photographic reconnaissance machine.*

△ *A Heinkel He 177 "Greif" (Griffin) goes up in flames after an R.A.F. raid. The 177 was Germany's attempt at a heavy bomber, but its advanced features made it very unreliable. Its most serious problems stemmed from the use of two engines coupled to drive a single propeller in each wing. The installation tended to overheat rapidly, resulting in mid-air fires.*

◁ *Quadruple 2-cm mounting.*

▷ *Focke Wulf Fw 200 "Kondor" in flight. Originally designed as a long-range airliner, the Fw 200 was pressed into war-time service as a maritime reconnaissance bomber, where its endurance and 3,300-lb bomb-load proved very useful. Relatively few were built, however.*

▽ *Classic fighter—the Messerschmitt Bf 109F. This model was the best flying machine of the series, with fully developed aerodynamics and engine, but the armament of one 20-mm and two 7.92-mm guns was deemed too light. The G model was fitted with heavier armament, but this increased weight and spoiled the type's clean lines, with a consequent harmful effect on flying qualities.*

▷ *Part of a myth: a line-up of Heinkel He 100D fighters. In fact only 12 production models of this rival to the Bf 109 were built, but German propaganda used photographs of these, painted in many different markings, successfully to fool Allied Intelligence that the type was in widespread service.*

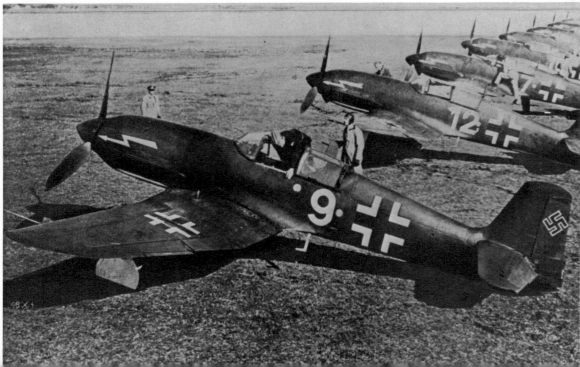

A.F. against small targets in "precision" raids. Flying in large "combat boxes", so that their defensive armament could cover each other, large numbers of B-17 Flying Fortresses raided important industrial targets in Germany and occupied Europe. But the tactics proved inadequate against the heavy armament and aggressive tactics of the German fighter arm—now composed principally of late model Bf 109's and the excellent Focke-Wulf Fw 190. Only with the arrival of long-range escort fighters, such as the Lockheed Lightning, North American Mustang, and Republic Thunderbolt, did day bombers reduce their losses. The American fighters also took a heavy toll of their German counterparts.

The basic choice of target for this vast bombing effort was not the best one, however. It was not until the last year of the war that the right one was found: the German transport system, and the industrial centres producing artificial rubber and petroleum products. The elimination of these produced almost immediate results—German troops could not be moved adequately, and even when they did arrive, transport and tanks were short of fuel. Moreover, many aircraft were grounded for lack of fuel.

At the tactical level, the Allies had produced a superb weapon. The origins of this magnificent force lay in the experiences of the British in North Africa, where the tactics of close co-operation between ground forces and heavily-armed fighter-bombers, such as the Hawker Hurricane IID, had been evolved. As in the early days of the war, ground troops were able to call in aircraft to halt enemy tanks for them or clear strong positions. This schooling was perfected in Italy, and by the time that the Allies invaded Normandy, the tactical air forces (equipped with medium bombers such as the American Mitchell and Marauder, and fighter-bombers such as the British Typhoon and later Tempest) were an all but irresistible weapon. The Germans found it impossible to move forces by day.

△ *The monstrous Messerschmitt Me 323 "Gigant" (Giant). Designed as a glider, six engines were later fitted to make this a very good transport aircraft, capable of carrying 130 troops.*

▽ *The excellent Ju 88, here represented as a night-fighter Ju 88G-6b, with radar and six 20-mm cannon, two firing upwards and forwards at an oblique angle.*

Sea warfare

The most dangerous threat to Great Britain's ability to stay in the war came from the U-boats of the Kriegsmarine, which waged a savage and courageous battle against the Royal Navy and Royal Air Force throughout the war. Although Germany's major U-boat offensive had been defeated by May 1943, the morale of her submariners still remained high, and with the new types of boat being developed towards the end of the war, another serious problem for the Allies could have arisen.

▽ *U-190 meets her end after the war. She was a Type IXC/40 boat (displacing 1,247 tons submerged, armed with 22 torpedoes and 42 mines in addition to her gun armament) which surrendered to the Canadians in May 1945. On October 21, 1947 she was sunk in a Canadian Navy exercise. She is seen here beginning to settle in the water after being hit by rockets from a Fairey Firefly.*

▷ *The business of submarine war: the view through the periscope of a U-boat.*

In the European Theatre of Operations (E.T.O.), the war at sea not only revolved around the Battle of the Atlantic but took in the fight for the Mediterranean and the north Russian convoy route. The English Channel, for centuries the arena for decisive sea battles, remained little more than a naval no-man's land sterilised by air power: a perilous route for German surface warships taking the most direct route to and from home waters. At night the Channel was the scene of bitter fighting between British and German light surface flotillas.

As in the Pacific theatre, naval strategy was dominated by air power in the E.T.O. Galland's efficient fighter screen defied every effort by the R.A.F. to prevent *Scharnhorst* and *Gneisenau* from escaping up-Channel in February 1942. The Luftwaffe savaged the British and French warships during the Norwegian campaign, but the aircraft of the British carrier *Glorious* were powerless to save her from destruction by the guns of *Scharnhorst* and *Gneisenau*–the first of the only two occasions in World War II when carriers were surprised by enemy surface warships (the second being at Leyte Gulf in October 1944). However, the British Fleet Air Arm cut the

Italian battle fleet down to size with its raid on Taranto in November 1940 and was thus instrumental in the winning of Cunningham's night victory over the Italian survivors at Matapan the following March.

The Luftwaffe earned ample revenge for Taranto and Matapan by the damage it dealt out to the British Mediterranean Fleet during the evacuations of Greece and Crete; and it had already become apparent that the struggle for Malta would be won or lost in the air, for Malta was like Midway atoll: an "unsinkable aircraft-carrier". Malta could never have held out without the aircraft repeatedly flown in by carriers steaming as far east as they dared from Gibraltar, with even the American *Wasp* lending a hand before sailing to her eventual doom off the Solomons. Out in the Atlantic the *Bismarck* would certainly have won through to Brest had she not been crippled by Fleet Air Arm Swordfish from the veteran *Ark Royal;* and the tragedy of P.Q.17 was as much the work of the Luftwaffe as of U-boat attacks. Finally *Tirpitz,* the one-vessel "fleet in being" which Dönitz had maintained for so long, was split open and capsized in Tromsö Fjord by the massive "Tallboy" bombs of

R.A.F. Lancasters.

Air power thus remained the *leitmotif* of the war at sea in the E.T.O., but several naval battles proved that traditional fighting qualities were far from obsolete at sea. Cunningham's victory at Matapan was one of the last classic night sea battles, while the interception of *Scharnhorst* off the North Cape on December 26, 1943 was the last fight between British and German capital ships. The indomitable manoeuvres of Vian's puny force of destroyers and light cruisers at "Second Sirte" in March 1942 saved a vital Malta convoy from a powerful Italian battle squadron. Deduction, luck, and frantic work in the engine-rooms just sufficed to get *Rodney* and *King George V* in position to pulverise *Bismarck* before their fuel ran out.

In the Far North, two particular operations illustrate the value of the "little ships" in World War II. The first came on the afternoon of May 1, 1942, when three of the tough new German destroyers tried to attack the return Russian convoy Q.P.11. The British destroyer escort was considerably out-gunned but its aggressive tactics induced the Germans to withdraw. A repeat performance came at the end of the year in the Battle of the

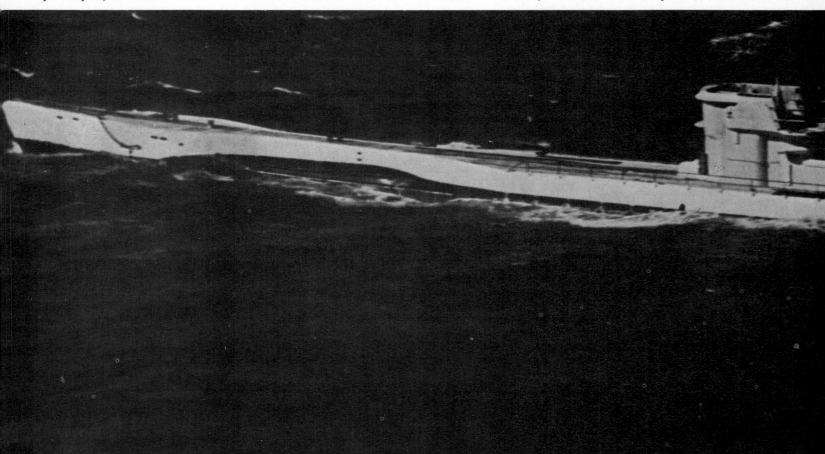

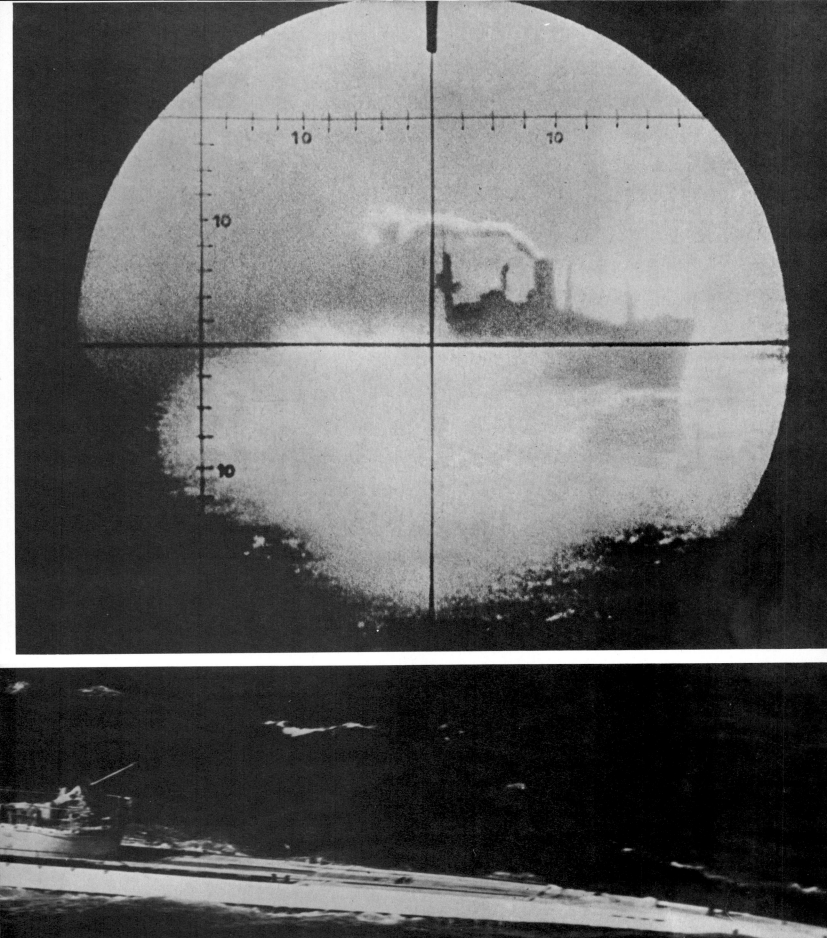

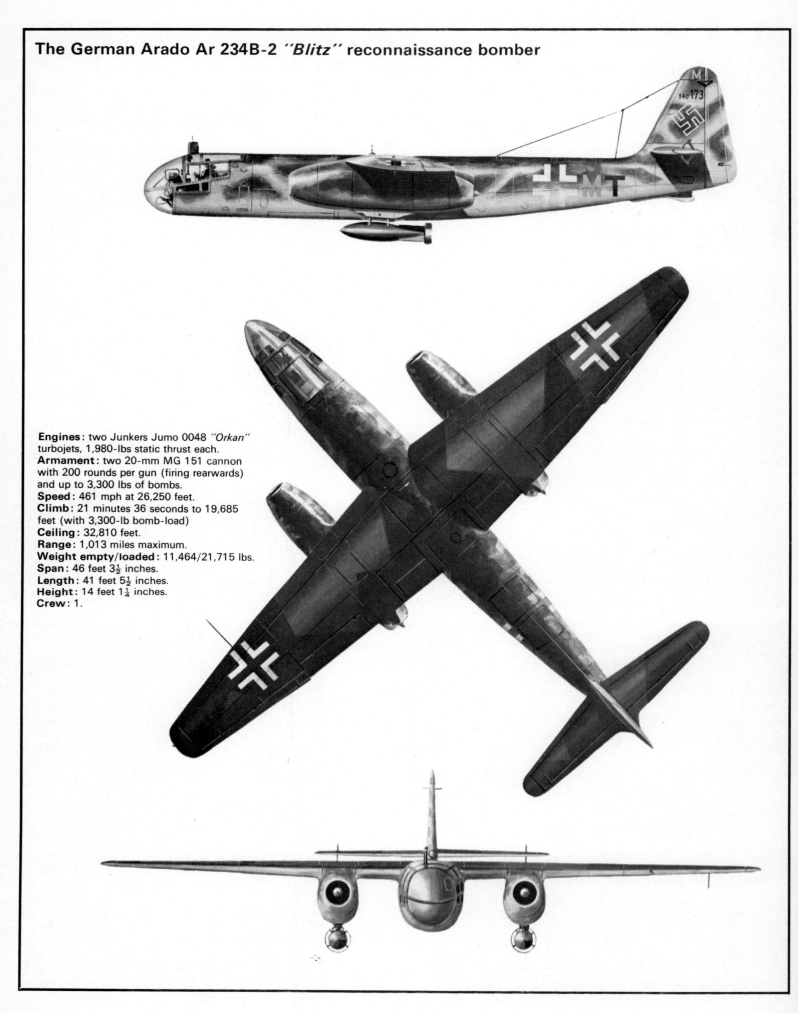

The German Arado Ar 234B-2 *"Blitz"* reconnaissance bomber

Engines: two Junkers Jumo 0048 *"Orkan"* turbojets, 1,980-lbs static thrust each.
Armament: two 20-mm MG 151 cannon with 200 rounds per gun (firing rearwards) and up to 3,300 lbs of bombs.
Speed: 461 mph at 26,250 feet.
Climb: 21 minutes 36 seconds to 19,685 feet (with 3,300-lb bomb-load)
Ceiling: 32,810 feet.
Range: 1,013 miles maximum.
Weight empty/loaded: 11,464/21,715 lbs.
Span: 46 feet 3½ inches.
Length: 41 feet 5½ inches.
Height: 14 feet 1¼ inches.
Crew: 1.

Barents Sea. Admiral Kummetz's *Regenbogen* ("Rainbow") plan caught Convoy J.W.51B between the heavy cruiser *Hipper* and the pocket-battleship *Lützow*. It was the closest the German surface fleet ever came to destroying a convoy to Russia, but again repeated "false torpedo attacks" by the British destroyers under Captain Sherbrooke caused the Germans to lose heart and withdraw.

In the war beneath the sea the German U-boat arm started the war promisingly when Prien's *U-47* sank the British battleship *Royal Oak* in Scapa Flow in October 1939, a month after Schuhardt's *U-29* had sunk the elderly carrier *Courageous* in the Western Approaches. But the next successes of the U-boats against the Royal Navy were scored in the Mediterranean: the *Barham* and *Ark Royal* in 1941 and *Eagle* the following August. The German U-boat operations in the Mediterranean, however, despite these successes, were a vital distraction from their main offensive in the Atlantic.

The Italian Navy began the war with a powerful fleet but its performance never came up to expectations. Of far more import-ance was the Italian development of the two-man "human torpedo". The successful use of these weapons at Alexandria in December 1941 sank the British battleships *Valiant* and *Queen Elizabeth* at their moorings and temporarily deprived the British Mediterranean Fleet of battleship support. This flash of Italian initiative led directly to the development of the two-man British "Chariot" (which failed even to reach the *Tirpitz*, let alone disable her) and the "X-craft" midget submarine (which did).

Storm-centre of the submarine war was, of course, the Atlantic.

△ *Germany's magnificent heavy cruiser* Prinz Eugen *arrives in Boston after the war. She was used in the atom bomb test at Bikini atoll on June 17, 1946 and sunk at Kwajalein on November 15, 1947.*

▽ *U-boats in Wilhelmshaven – at the extreme left is the Type IXD/2 U-883 (surrendered at Wilhelmsaven and scuttled in the Atlantic in 1946) with three Type VIIC boats. Together the Types VII and IX boats formed the backbone of Germany's ocean raiding force.*

△ Preparing the minesweeping gear on board a British minesweeper. The Germans produced several very tricky mines at the beginning of the war, but lost their potential advantage in this field by using new types as they began to come off the production lines, rather than waiting to use them en masse to swamp the unprepared British counter-measures.

▷ The British also used mines to good effect where what little German sea transport there was had to operate, such as along the coast of Norway. Seen here are German motor minesweepers off the Lofoten Islands.

Here the Germans began with brilliant successes by individual U-boat aces – Prien, Schepke, and Kretschmer being the most famous names – and rapidly evolved the more methodical "wolf-pack" concerted tactics. To this the Allies retaliated with "hunter-killer" groups, adopting the American voice-contact T.B.S. ("talk-between-ships"), "Hedgehog" projectors for firing spreads of depth-charges, and the all-important "Huff-Duff" (High Frequency Direction Finding) for tracking down and counter-attacking lurking U-boats. Of paramount importance, however, was the gradual extension of air cover to screen the entire Atlantic route – "bridging the Black Gap", as the process was known. Stopgap escort warships as typified by the "Flower" class corvettes were pressed into service and did sterling work until the more sophisticated anti-submarine frigates could join the fray.

British submarines in the Western Approaches had a disappointing war. They failed to prevent the escape of the German squadron from Brest, and were never given a fair shot at either *Tirpitz* or *Scharnhorst* in the Far North. But in the Mediterranean they were the spearhead of the British Malta-based attacks on the Axis supply-route to North Africa. The most famous of many British submarine aces in the Mediterranean was Wanklyn of the *Upholder*. Later, when the Axis bombardment of Malta had vir-

tually neutralised the base and its fall seemed imminent, submarines were pressed into service to run in supplies for the hard-pressed garrison.

Sea power, one of the most traditional weapons of strategy, was remorselessly affected by 20th Century technology in World War II. To a large extent, as we have seen, it was forced to dance to the tune of air power. Radar and other electronic aids meant that battles were brought on by more accuracy than that supplied by the naked eye. But at all levels of the war at sea, from the biggest fleet action to destroyer duels and skirmishes between E-boats and M.T.B.s, the human element remained the decisive factor. Radar could locate. Radio could communicate. Powerful engines could close the range. But when it came to the sticking-point all that mattered was the application of skilled men wielding the tools of their trade despite the dangers of battle. And there can be little doubt that the men of the fighting ships found it easier to endure than did the crews of the merchantmen who owed their lives to their escorts. On the long, slow convoys whose safe arrival decided the outcome of the war, the dedication and courage of the merchant seamen played no less a part. Together with the fighting seamen, they proved that the best warship in the world must always be useless in the absence of seamanship and courage.

▷ *British submarines did not have the same scope of action as their German counterparts, as the merchant navies of the Axis powers were considerably smaller than those of the Allies. Nevertheless, British boats won some notable successes, in particular against the Italians in the Mediterranean, and also performed useful services in the delivery and retrieval of agents and raiding parties. Seen here is the conning tower of the S-class* Seraph. *The class as a whole proved an excellent design.*

▽ *The British cruiser* Belfast, *one of the two ships in the third variation of the* Southampton *class. She displaced some 10,000 tons and was armed with twelve 6-inch guns, with which she supported the landings in Normandy very successfully.*

The British Gloster Meteor III interceptor fighter

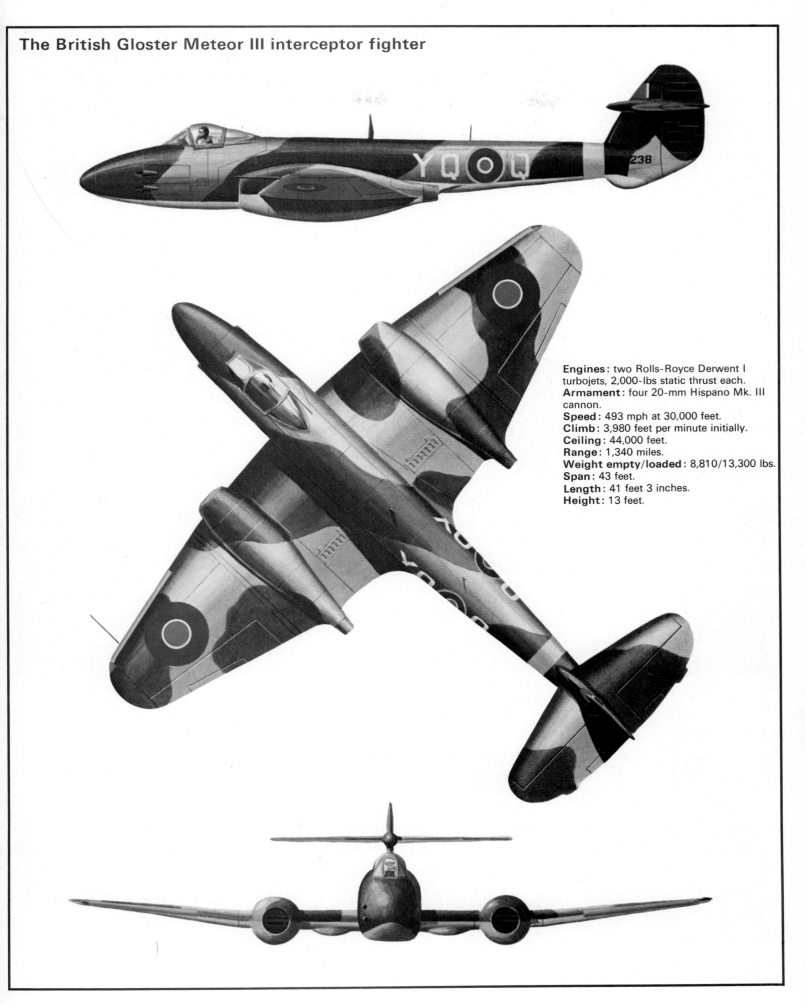

Engines: two Rolls-Royce Derwent I turbojets, 2,000-lbs static thrust each.
Armament: four 20-mm Hispano Mk. III cannon.
Speed: 493 mph at 30,000 feet.
Climb: 3,980 feet per minute initially.
Ceiling: 44,000 feet.
Range: 1,340 miles.
Weight empty/loaded: 8,810/13,300 lbs.
Span: 43 feet.
Length: 41 feet 3 inches.
Height: 13 feet.

2490

The German battleship *Tirpitz*, younger sister of the celebrated *Bismarck*, was possibly the most important single factor in the Royal Navy's planning from her move to Norway at the beginning of 1942 to her loss at the end of 1944. As long as she lay poised to foray out into the Atlantic like *Bismarck*, powerful forces had to be kept in the Home Fleet to deal with her. This goes a long way towards explaining Cunningham's acute shortage of heavy vessels in the Mediterranean and the slow growth of the Eastern Fleet. Offensive measures also cost Britain dear: the raid on St. Nazaire (to destroy the only Atlantic dock capable of accommodating her), a midget submarine attack on September 23, 1943, naval air strikes on April 3, August 22, and August 24, 1944 (the first and last of which damaged her), and Bomber Command attacks on September 15 and November 12, 1944 with 12,000-lb "Tallboy" bombs. The first R.A.F. raid caused damage that prevented *Tirpitz* putting out to sea, and the second capsized her at her moorings at Tromsö.

△ △ ◁ *Tirpitz* in her lair.
△ ◁ *The raid of April 3 by Fleet Air Arm Barracuda dive-bombers. Forty-two aircraft took part, scoring 14 hits and killing 122 crew.*
◁ ◁ *Rudder and propeller shaft bracket after the capsizing.*
△ *Bottom up in Tromsö fjord.*
◁ *Salvage work.*

The end of Germany's massive U-boat effort.
△ The U-boat pens at Finken-wärde. These had been built over a period of four years by 1,700 slave labourers, and were blown up by 32 tons of captured German bombs detonated inside them.
▷ The ruin of the U-boat pens in Kiel.

▽ Inside the pens at Finken-wärde after their destruction.

POTSDAM
THE LAST CONFERENCE

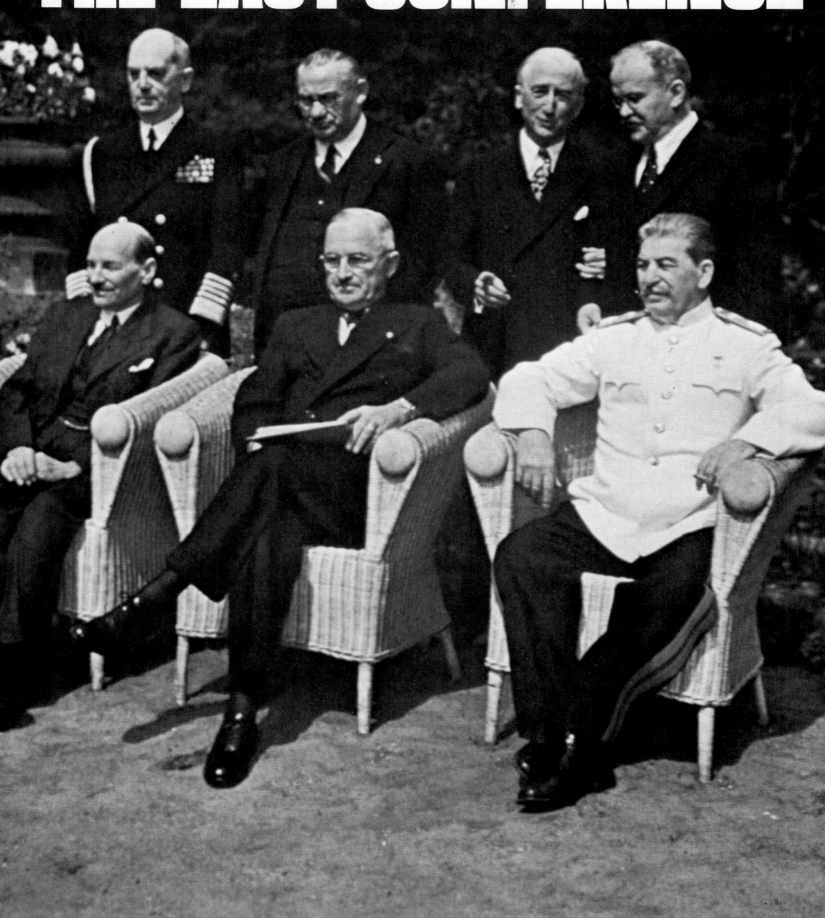

In the early days of May 1945, Prime Minister Churchill was in a profoundly worried mood. True, the struggle against Hitler was finished when Germany surrendered on May 8. But Churchill could not join fully in the rejoicing of the London crowds on V.E. Day. Japan was still unconquered, and now the West was faced with a new threat: the tide of Soviet imperialism was running unchecked across Eastern Europe. Communist or pro-Communist puppet governments had been set up by the Russians in Bulgaria and in Rumania in violation of the Yalta agreement, and Western news reports were suppressed. "An iron curtain is drawn down upon their front," Churchill wrote on May 12, "We do not know what is going on behind."

The Prime Minister felt that it was necessary to have a showdown with Stalin immediately. The United States were preparing to withdraw their troops in Germany back to the predetermined occupation zone. This would give the Russians another large chunk of Germany, 300-400 miles long and 120 miles wide. "This would be an event which, if it occured, would be one of the most melancholy in history," Churchill wrote. The territory under Russian control would include "all the great capitals of middle Europe including Berlin, Vienna, Budapest, Belgrade, Bucharest and Sofia." Only Greece would be saved. If Churchill and President Truman did not confront Stalin before the American withdrawal, the Western Allies would have little bargaining power. As early as May 6, therefore, Churchill sent an urgent telegram to Truman asking for a conference of the "Big Three" as soon as possible.

Truman agreed that the Three should meet soon, but said that he himself could not attend until July, after Congress had approved

his new budget programme. He had been president for less than a month, and did not share Churchill's dread of Russian domination in eastern Europe. But Truman agreed that a conference of the three heads of state would help clear up outstanding differences over the procedure for drafting peace treaties, the occupation of Germany, and the question of reparations, as well as the eastern Europe question. He suggested that the conference might meet in Alaska, or perhaps Vienna, and that he and Churchill should arrive separately, to avoid giving Stalin the impression that

Page 2493: *The last "Big Three" Conference, at Potsdam in July 1945. But this time there were two new faces–Clement Attlee of Great Britain and Harry S Truman of the U.S.*
△ ◁ ◁ *German civilians loot a liquor store.*
△ ◁ *German girls make their way home with the spoils from a looted distillery in Lippstadt.*
◁ *With the strengthening of law enforcement in the months after Germany's surrender, black marketeers found the going more difficult, as these women have found to their cost.*
△ *Hitler's portrait comes down.*

△ ◁ *The team that steered Britain to victory, seen on May 7, 1945. Standing: Major-General L. C. Horris (left) and General Sir Hastings Ismay; seated, left to right: Air Chief-Marshal Sir Charles Portal, Winston Churchill, Field-Marshal Sir Alan Brooke, and Admiral of the Fleet Sir Andrew Cunningham.*

△ *But while the Allies celebrated V. E. Day, in Germany the position was somewhat different. Although most were glad that the war was over, there was now the heart-breaking job of picking up the pieces – under Allied occupation.*

◁ ◁ *Not least of Germany's problems was the reconstruction of industry, so that she could pay her way in the world, after the ministrations of Allied strategic bombing.*

◁ *The new, non-Nazi Germany in the making: German children on their way to school under the watchful eyes of one British and two Belgian soldiers.*

Overleaf: *The shell of Cologne.*

Apart from the moral and social problems of rebuilding Germany, there was also the vast effort required to clear up the actual physical debris of war before reconstruction work could start. The best tool for the job was manpower, and Germany's people weighed into the problem with a vengeance – not least of all because their food rations were dependent on it.

△ *Rationalising the skeleton of gutted Dresden.*

△▷ *A Berliner in the old business quarter, now in the Russian sector.*

▷ *Body count in Dresden, under the supervision of Russian officers. But how could an accurate figure be arrived at when thousands of bodies were reduced to nothing but fine dust by the fire-storms?*

the Anglo-Saxon leaders were "ganging up" on him.

Stalin himself suggested that the meeting take place near Berlin, and agreed with Truman that July 15 should be the date.

The codename for the conference was to be "Terminal"; each delegation would have a separate headquarters at Babelsberg, a suburb of Berlin just south of Potsdam. The meetings themselves would take place in the Cecilienhof Palace, a former home of the German Crown Prince. The heads of state would be accompanied by their foreign ministers and other top officials, but the press would not be invited.

As the date of the conference approached, President Truman and his staff produced dozens of notes, agendas, and memoranda for their use at Potsdam. Churchill, on the other hand, did not set his plans down on paper, but took a short holiday.

The two Western leaders both

arrived at Babelsberg on July 15. Churchill drove to the house that was to be his headquarters, a large home in the former film colony of Germany. President Truman's residence, near Churchill's, was similar and soon became known as the "Little White House". It lacked screens, however, and the American delegation was to suffer mosquito bites for the first few days until the weather cooled. Stalin's house was about a mile away, much closer to the actual conference centre – the Russians had arranged that.

The Soviet leader, recently promoted from Marshal to Generalissimo, arrived on July 17, and the first conference session took place that evening. Truman was named chairman, at Stalin's suggestion. He immediately proposed that a Council of Foreign Ministers be set up to draft peace treaties and deal with other problems after the end of hostilities.

This proposal was quickly approved, although there was some debate over whether China and France should be included.

The prompt agreement on the first proposal raised hopes that other issues could also be resolved without difficulty. This optimism was soon dispelled as the three leaders debated the situation in eastern Europe. Churchill and Truman denounced the Russian violation of the Yalta terms in setting up puppet governments in the East. Instead of allowing all democratic groups to join the caretaker governments, the Soviets had restricted participation to those known to be friendly to Moscow. There was also evidence that the Soviets did not intend to hold free and unfettered elections. Then there was Stalin's demand for reparations from Italy. The Western leaders wanted special treaty arrangements for Italy, which had eventually joined the Allies and promised help

▷ *French prisoners-of-war discuss how best to get home to France.*

△ *While the Americans and the British were restricted in their social activities by non-fraternisation orders, no such worries hindered Russian soldiers.*

▷▷ *One of the legion of female "rubble workers" of Berlin takes her meagre mid-day meal.*

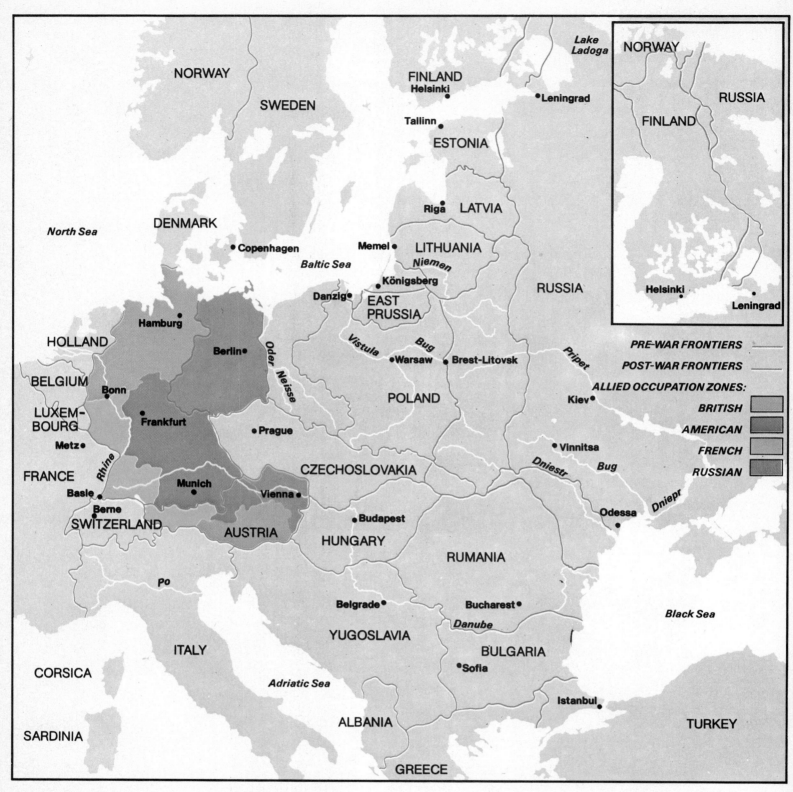

NORWAY

SWEDEN

FINLAND
Helsinki

Lake Ladoga

Leningrad

NORWAY

RUSSIA

FINLAND

Helsinki

Leningrad

Tallinn

ESTONIA

North Sea

DENMARK

Copenhagen

Baltic Sea

Riga

LATVIA

Memel

LITHUANIA

Niemen

RUSSIA

PRE-WAR FRONTIERS

POST-WAR FRONTIERS

ALLIED OCCUPATION ZONES:

HOLLAND

Hamburg

Berlin

Königsberg

Danzig

EAST PRUSSIA

Vistula

Bug

BRITISH

BELGIUM

Bonn

Oder

Neisse

Warsaw

Brest-Litovsk

Pripet

AMERICAN

LUXEM-BOURG

Frankfurt

POLAND

Kiev

FRENCH

Metz

Prague

RUSSIAN

Rhine

Munich

CZECHOSLOVAKIA

Vinnitsa

Dniestr

Bug

FRANCE

Basle

Vienna

Dniepr

Berne

SWITZERLAND

AUSTRIA

Budapest

Odessa

Po

HUNGARY

RUMANIA

Belgrade

Bucharest

Black Sea

Danube

ITALY

YUGOSLAVIA

BULGARIA

CORSICA

Adriatic Sea

Sofia

Istanbul

SARDINIA

ALBANIA

TURKEY

GREECE

△ *Post-war Europe.*

△ ▷ *and* ▷ *The non-fraternisation order is lifted. The order on British troops had been imposed before the end of the war, but on June 12 the order was lifted to allow soldiers to speak to and play with children, and from July 1 the troops were allowed to speak to Germans in public places. Finally, in September, the rest of the ban was lifted. The only things not permitted were accommodation in German homes and marriage.*

against Japan; Stalin would not grant favours to Italy which would not be shared by Hungary, Rumania, and Bulgaria. The Three did not reach a definite agreement on these questions at Potsdam, merely referring them to the attention of the new Council of Foreign Ministers. Similar decisions were made concerning the question of what "war booty" each Ally could legitimately confiscate, and the Soviet desire for trusteeship over some of the colonies of the

defeated Axis powers.

The conference was interrupted temporarily on July 25. Churchill and the Leader of the Opposition, Clement Attlee, returned to Britain to await the outcome of the recent general election. The actual voting had taken place on July 5, but the final results were not known until the 26th. Churchill had brought Attlee to the conference to ensure continuity in the British position, regardless of the outcome of the election, and on one occasion,

with Attlee at his side, Churchill had toasted "The Leader of the Opposition—whoever he may be." On July 26, the result was announced: the voters had chosen Attlee's Labour Government. Two days later, Prime Minister Attlee returned to Potsdam and took his place beside Truman and Stalin.

The last four meetings at Potsdam were concerned with Germany. All agreed that the nation must be denazified and disarmed. In the words of the official com-

The damage to Germany was comprehensive, embracing industry, urban areas, transport, and historic monuments.

△ ◁ ◁ Cologne.

△ ◁ The Propaganda Ministry in Berlin.

△ Combat engineers of the U.S. Army salvage steel from the Fallersleben factory, which had been turned from Volkswagen to V-1 production during the war.

◁ ◁ The Foreign Ministry in Berlin, pictured on August 21, 1945.

◁ The Henschel aircraft engine factory at Altenbaun near Kassel, completely destroyed by two U.S.A.A.F. raids.

△ *Refugees in Vienna's main station.*
◁ *A measure of comfort: released after 13 years in a Russian camp, Count Bismarck greets his mother. Years in Russian labour camps was the fate that awaited many thousands of German fighting men taken by the Russians.*
▷ *Cologne's Hohenzollern Bridge across the Rhine.*

muniqué, "all German land, sea and air forces, the SS, SA, SD and Gestapo, with all their organisations, staffs and institutions, including the General Staff, Officers' Corps, Reserve Corps, military schools, war veterans' organisations, and all other military and quasi-military organisations, together with all clubs and associations which serve to keep alive the military tradition in Germany, are to be completely and finally abolished . . ." War criminals were to be arrested and tried, and high-ranking Nazis interned. All more-than-nominal members of the Nazi Party were to be removed from public office and positions of responsibility in private undertakings and enterprises.

The question of reparations was more difficult. The Three

had previously agreed to treat Germany as an economic unit, and reparations were to be drawn from the nation as a whole. But the Western leaders had learned that the Red Army was confiscating all manner of goods (including household furniture) in the Russian-occupied zone. No agreement could be reached on the value of these goods, and this made it impossible to make a fair division of reparations. This thorny problem was ingeniously solved by an American proposal: each occupying power should collect its share of reparations from its own zone of occupation, rather than from Germany as a whole. This idea was accepted, with provisions for trading coal and food supplies in the Russian zone for industrial equipment from the Western areas.

The last great question at Potsdam concerned the Polish border. It had been agreed already that the Russians were to receive Polish territory east of the Curzon Line, and that Poland would eventually receive German territory in compensation.

No decision had been made as to where this western boundary would be fixed. But the Russians had unilaterally transferred a huge chunk of conquered German territory, as far west as the Oder and Western Neisse, to the Polish Government which Churchill described as the "ardent puppet" of the Soviet Union. This meant that the richest agricultural and coal-producing area of Germany was not to be included in the debate on reparations, and millions of hungry Germans would have to be repatriated to the western zones.

The most important decision at Potsdam was not, strictly speaking, part of the conference. On July 17, Churchill had been told that the test at Alamogordo, New Mexico, had been successful: the atomic bomb was a reality. Truman and Churchill agreed that a final opportunity must be given to the Japanese to surrender. If they refused, the new weapon must be used to end the war. On July 26, therefore, the two leaders, together with China's Chiang Kai-shek – the Soviet Union was not then at war with Japan – issued the Potsdam Declaration. "We call upon the Government of Japan to proclaim now the unconditional surrender of all the Japanese armed forces," the declaration said. ". . . The alternative for Japan is prompt and utter destruction."

△ ◁ *Justice is meted out: the scene in a Vienna court as the sentences on four men convicted of murdering over 100 Jews are passed. The man crying has been given eight years' gaol. The other three were sentenced to death.*
◁ *Cossacks serving with the Wehrmacht, rounded up by the British in Austria.*
△ *The Yugoslav partisan forces pull out of Klagenfurt after reaching agreement with the British about occupation zones and the fact that the Yugoslavs had none.*

TITO

AND THE YUGOSLAV PARTISANS

On April 17, 1941, the Yugoslav Army capitulated to the Germans. Resistance to the Axis forces began early, but it was divided between Mihailović's royalists and Tito's Communists. Tito formed a nation-wide resistance group, known as the Partisans, and played a major rôle in freeing Yugoslavia of the German occupation forces.

Tito's long term aim was the Communist control of a united Yugoslavia. Communist policy at this time was directed from Russia, but the practical organisation was left to Tito. The party organisation he had set up just before the war, which covered all regions of Yugoslavia, had now been disrupted. In April and May, he summoned the Yugoslav Communist Party Central Committee to meetings to decide on a plan of campaign. Orders went out to Communists in all parts of the country to collect secret stockpiles of weapons. The call for the revolt of the Yugoslav peoples did not come until July 4, however, after the Germans had attacked Russia, and this led to an intensive campaign of attacks all over the country. Tito had sent trained men out to the country, usually to the regions where they were born, to lead the uprisings.

The task of organising and co-

◁ *Tito, head of the Yugoslav partisan movement, with an aide in the mountains of northern Yugoslavia in 1945.*

▽ *Partisans prepare to blow the bridge at Nikšić, 40 miles east of Dubrovnik.*

▽ *Men of a Croatian Proletarian Brigade in May 1942.*
▷ *German infantry crouch behind a* leichter Panzerspähwagen Sd.Kfz 222 *armoured car in action against Bosnian partisans.*
▽▷ *There was no sexual discrimination among the partisans: this girl was a front line soldier wounded in the field after killing 20 Germans.*

ordinating the dispersed groups of partisans was difficult and dangerous, calling for a high degree of ability. Tito proved himself equal to it.

Clandestine operations were to be maintained in enemy-occupied towns, while a guerrilla war of movement was waged against the Germans in the countryside, with the aim of tying down as many enemy troops as possible over as wide an area as possible. The Germans could not hope to control the whole of the countryside, and Tito instructed his forces to avoid direct clashes with a superior enemy, and, if necessary, to retreat before the Germans.

Tito's efforts were extremely successful, and the Germans were driven out of much of Serbia by mid-September. Partisan activity appealed to the national spirit, and to the love of freedom of many who were not Communists. Support for the revolts also increased after General Keitel ordered the execution of 50-100 Communists in reprisal for the death of any German soldier.

Tito's attention was diverted from the enemy when he tried and failed to reach a compromise with Mihailović, the leader of the other important resistance group, the Četniks. In the struggle between the two men to gain control of the complete resistance movement, open clashes occurred. This dis-

△ *Appalling terrain over which to fight, but it was the Yugoslavs' country and they knew how to use it in their struggle against the Germans. Here a German soldier watches a Stuka bombardment of a suspected partisan stronghold.*
▷ *Partisans unload supplies flown into Nikśić airfield by the British from Italy.*
▷▷ *Wounded partisans being evacuated to the mountains to recuperate.*

sension allowed the Germans to move in again. They launched their first attack in western Serbia in September 1941, and by December, most of Serbia was under Axis control.

At this time, enlistment to the partisans was on a voluntary basis and detachments had been local units fighting to defend their own home regions. Tito now needed a stable, trained army and

strike force to execute the war of movement. Accordingly, the 1st Proletarian Shock Brigade was formed in December 1941, and the 2nd during March the following year. By the end of November 1942, Tito's army had 28 brigades, each with 3-4,000 men and women. This People's Liberation Army was used increasingly for offensive action, and had its own training school, organisations for women and youths, and also a naval detachment. Each brigade had a political commissar as well as a commanding officer. Although the brigades were short of ammunition and uniforms, the partisans were very disciplined. All their supplies were paid for, and a high moral standard governed relations between men and women partisans.

Not until late 1943 did the Allies send him aid, and before that, Tito and the partisans had to fight off five German offensives. From the outset, the enemy embarked on a policy of deliberate extermination of the wounded and the sick as a weapon against the fighting morale of the rebel bands. This was contrary to the tradition of care of the wounded implicit in the code of Balkan guerrilla warfare. Tito's order was to save the wounded at all costs. As they were waging a war of mobility, the sick and the wounded had to accompany the army on the move.

By May 1944, Tito had the full support of the Allies, and the Germans were in full retreat by the end of August. In March 1945, Tito set up a provisional government with himself as Prime Minister.

1944

December

16. The Battle of the Bulge. German 5th and 6th *Panzerarmee* under Rundstedt counter-attack U.S. 1st and 9th Armies in the Ardennes.
17. Allied reinforcements move towards the Ardennes.
19. German column reaches the Houffalize and Bastogne area. Montgomery takes over the Allied forces to the north of the Ardennes, Bradley those to the south.
20. Germans reach the Stavelot and Noville areas.
21. Germans besiege Bastogne.
22. Final German attempt to push to the Meuse.
25. Churchill and Eden arrive in Athens. German tanks halted four miles from the Meuse.
26. U.S. tanks push through to relieve Bastogne. Churchill meets Greek politicians.
27. Budapest surrounded. Corridor to Bastogne opened by U.S. 3rd Army.
29. Street fighting in Budapest.
30. 14th Army takes Kaduma. Germans attack Bastogne corridor and halt U.S. attacks on Houffalize.
31. R.A.F. Mosquitoes attack Oslo Gestapo H.Q.

1945

January

1. In last major attack of the war the Luftwaffe sends 800 aircraft to attack airfields in France, Belgium, and Holland.
2. Germans counter-attack at Budapest. Admiral Sir Bertram Ramsay killed in air crash.
3. U.S. 1st Army counter-attacks in Ardennes salient.
4. 8th Army attacks at Senio. *Kamikaze* and conventional attacks on invasion convoys in Lingayen Gulf.
7. 14th Army reaches Shwebo, occupies Kinu.
9. U.S. 6th Army lands at Lingayen Gulf on Luzon Island.
11. Russians enter Warsaw.
12. Russians begin winter offensive in south Poland.
14. Bridgeheads established across the Irrawaddy north of Mandalay.
16. U.S. 1st and 3rd Armies link up at Houffalize to eliminate the Ardennes salient.
17. Germans evacuate Warsaw.
18. Germans break through Russian lines to link up with Budapest garrison.
19. Russians take Tilsit and Kraków.

20. French 1st Army attacks in Vosges to destroy the Colmar Pocket.
22. Burma road reopened.
25. Russians cross the Oder near Breslau and Steinau.
26. Russians take Auschwitz.
28. Final destruction of the Ardennes salient. Russians enter Pomerania.
31. Pre-Yalta conference at Malta: Churchill, Eden, and Stettinius meet with the Combined Chiefs-of-Staff.

February

. U.S. 7th Army reaches the Siegfried Line.
. Roosevelt arrives at Malta.
. Yalta Conference opens. U.S. 1st Army captures the first Rur dam.
. Australians land on New Britain.
. Russians cross the upper Oder.
. Germans blow the Schwammanuel dam floodgates.
. British and Canadians break through Siegfried Line and reach the Rhine.
11. Destruction of German garrison in Budapest.
12. Yalta Conference ends.
13. 14th Army establishes bridgeheads over the Irrawaddy south of Mandalay. R.A.F. attacks Dresden: huge civilian casualties. Budapest falls to Russians.
14. U.S.A.A.F. raids Dresden. U.S. 6th Army begins operations on Bataan peninsula.
15. Russians drive towards Danzig and encircle Breslau.
16. Air and naval bombardment of Iwo Jima begins.
19. U.S. Marines land on strategic island of Iwo Jima.
22. Operation "Clarion": attack by 10,000 Allied aircraft on central German road and rail communications.
23. Marines take Mount Suribachi on Iwo Jima.
27. Marines secure second air strip on Iwo Jima.
28. Corregidor declared secure.

March

. U.S. 9th Army captures Mönchen-Gladbach.
. U.S. 3rd Army captures Trier.

4. British and Canadians take Vynen and Apeldoorn. U.S. 3rd Army establishes bridgehead on the Kyll.
5. Cologne captured. Russians approach Stettin.
7. U.S. 1st Army crosses the Rhine over the Remagen railway bridge.
8. Americans enter Bonn.
10. B-29 fire-raid destroys over $16\frac{1}{2}$ acres of Tokyo.
13. 14th Army captures Maymo, cutting Japanese escape route from Mandalay.
16. Iwo Jima declared secure.
17. U.S. 3rd Army captures Koblenz.
30. U.S. 7th Army occupies Saarbrücken. Nagoya hit by B-29 incendiary raid.
22. Russians besiege Danzig and Gdynia. U.S. 5th Division crosses the Rhine.
23. British 2nd and Canadian 1st Armies begin Rhine crossing.
24. British and U.S. airborne divisions drop near Wesel and link up with British infantry.
25. U.S. 3rd Army crosses the Rhine, captures Darmstadt.
27. U.S. 1st and 3rd Armies link up near Koblenz. U.S. forces take Wiesbaden. Last V-2 lands in England.
28. Allied objective switched from Berlin to Leipzig. British 2nd Army begins drive to the Elbe.
29. U.S. 3rd Army captures Frankfurt. Bombardment of Okinawa begins.
30. Russians capture Danzig.

April

1. U.S. 1st and 9th Armies complete encirclement of Ruhr, linking at Lippstadt. Okinawa invaded by U.S. 10th Army.
2. 8th Army attacks between Lake Commachio and the Adriatic.
4. Hungary is cleared of Germans. Resistance increases on Okinawa.

7. First escort for B-29's over Japan. Battle of East China Sea, Japanese lose the *Yamato*.

9. Russians take Königsberg fortress. R.A.F. bombers sink the *Admiral Scheer* at Kiel.

12. Death of President Roosevelt; Harry Truman sworn in as President.

15. Canadians reach the sea in north Holland, Arnhem captured. Malinovsky takes Vienna.

18. Ruhr pocket is neutralised; 317,000 prisoners taken.

20. Nuremberg falls to the U.S. 7th Army.

22. Russians begin pincer attack on Berlin.

23. 8th and 5th Armies reach the Po.

24. Red Army forces link up in Berlin. Dachau concentration camp liberated.

25. U.S. 1st Army patrols make contact with Russians near Torgau. R.A.F. bombs Berchtesgaden.

28. Mussolini captured near Swiss border and killed by partisans.

29. German army representatives sign terms of unconditional surrender at Caserta; hostilities cease on May 2. Hitler nominates Dönitz as his successor and marries Eva Braun.

30. Hitler commits suicide in the Chancellery bunker. Russians reach the Reichstag building in Berlin.

May

2. Russians hold Berlin. Final raid in Europe, R.A.F. Mosquitoes hit Kiel.

3. Montgomery meets German envoys at Lüneburg Heath. Hamburg surrenders. Indians reach Rangoon.

4. Germans agree to surrender in Holland, Denmark, and north-west Germany.

7. Jodl signs the instrument of unconditional surrender of all German forces at Eisenhower's H.Q. at Rheims.

8. Churchill and Truman declare V.E. Day.